CoRE 2017

Read On...Life Stories

D0555929

Read On...Life Stories

Reading Lists for Every Taste

Rosalind Reisner

Read On Series
Barry Trott, Series Editor

LIBRARIES UNLIMITED
An Imprint of ABC-CLIO, LLC

A B C ☕ C L I O

Santa Barbara, California • Denver, Colorado • Oxford, England

Library of Congress Cataloging-in-Publication Data

Reisner, Rosalind.
    Read on— life stories : reading lists for every taste / Rosalind Reisner.
        p. cm. — (Read on series)
    Includes bibliographical references and index.
    ISBN 978-1-59158-766-8 (acid-free paper)   1. Autobiography—
Bibliography.   2. Readers' advisory services—United States.   3. Public
libraries—United States—Book lists.   I. Title.

    Z5301.R45   2009
    [CT25]
    016.92—dc22   2009023222

13   12   11   10   09   1   2   3   4   5

This book is also available on the World Wide Web as an eBook.
Visit www.abc-clio.com for details.

ABC-CLIO, LLC
130 Cremona Drive, P.O. Box 1911
Santa Barbara, California 93116-1911

This book is printed on acid-free paper ∞
Manufactured in the United States of America

Contents

Series Foreword

Welcome to Libraries Unlimited's Read On series of fiction and nonfiction genre guides for readers' advisors and for readers. The Read On series introduces readers and those who work with them to new ways of looking at books, genres, and reading interests.

Over the past decade, readers' advisory services have become vital in public libraries. A quick glance at the schedule of any library conference at the state or national level will reveal a wealth of programs on various aspects of connecting readers to books they will enjoy. Working with unfamiliar genres or types of reading can be a challenge, particularly for those new to the field. Equally, readers may find it a bit overwhelming to look for books outside their favorite authors and preferred reading interests. The titles in the Read On series offer you a new way to approach reading:

- they introduce you a broad sampling of materials available in a given genre;
- they offer you new directions to explore in a genre—through appeal features and unconventional topics;
- they help readers' advisors better understand and navigate genres with which they are less familiar;
- and they provide reading lists that you can use to create quick displays, include on your library Web sites and in the library newsletter, or to hand out to readers.

The lists in the Read On series are arranged in sections based on appeal characteristics—story, character, setting, and language (as described in Joyce G. Saricks's *Readers' Advisory Service in the Public Library,* 3d ed., ALA Editions, 2005), with a fifth section on mood. These are hidden elements of a book that attract readers. Remember that a book can have multiple appeal factors; and sometimes readers are drawn to a particular book for several factors, while other times for only one. In the Read On lists, titles are placed according to their primary appeal characteristics, and then put into a list that reflects common reading interests. So if you are working with a reader who loves fantasy that features quests for magical objects or a reader who is interested in memoirs with a strong sense of place, you will be able to find a list of titles whose main appeal centers around this search. Each list indicates a title that is an especially good starting place for readers, an exemplar of that appeal characteristic.

Story is perhaps the most basic appeal characteristic. It relates to the plot of the book—what are the elements of the tale? Is the emphasis more on the people or the situations? Is the story action focused or more interior? Is it funny? Scary?

Many readers are drawn to the books they love by the characters. The character appeal reflects such aspects as whether there are lots of characters or only a single main character; are the characters easily recognizable types? Do the characters grow and change over the course of the story? What are the characters' occupations?

Setting covers a range of elements that might appeal to readers. What is the time period or geographic locale of the tale? How much does the author describe the surroundings of the story? Does the reader feel as though he or she is "there," when reading the book? Are there special features such as the monastic location of Ellis Peters's Brother Cadfael mysteries or the small town setting of Jan Karon's Mitford series?

Although not traditionally considered appeal characteristic, mood is important to readers as well. It relates to how the author uses the tools of narrative—language, pacing, story, and character—to create a feeling for the work. Mood can be difficult to quantify because the reader brings his or her own feelings to the story as well. Mood really asks how does the book make the reader feel? Creepy? Refreshed? Joyful? Sad?

Finally, the language appeal brings together titles where the author's writing style draws the reader. This can be anything from a lyrical prose style with lots of flourishes to a spare use of language à la Hemingway. Humor, snappy dialog, wordplay, recipes, and other language elements all have the potential to attract readers.

Dig into these lists. Use them to find new titles and authors in a genre that you love, or as a guide to expand your knowledge of a new type of writing...Above all, read, enjoy, and remember—never apologize for your reading tastes!

Barry Trott
Series Editor

Introduction

Why do people write life stories? And why are we so keen on reading them? Telling life stories is as old as the cave paintings of the Stone Age and as new as YouTube. We tell our stories to friends, lovers, children, therapists, and even strangers if they'll listen. We hear other people's stories, absorb them into our own lives, and pass them on.

Writing down our life stories helps us see a narrative thread in our lives, reflect on the consequences of events and find coherence, maybe even redemption or closure. But after we write, we need to share what's written. Life stories, memoirs, autobiographies—whatever term we use—have been a wildly popular nonfiction genre for the past 20 years. In the 1990s, Frank McCourt's *Angela's Ashes* and Mary Karr's *The Liar's Club,* among others, sparked an enthusiastic response among readers that has yet to subside. Memoirs have elbowed their way into book discussion groups. Issues of truthfulness in memoirs have become front page and talk show news. Elsewhere, reality TV shows, social networking sites on the Internet, blogs, oral history organizations like StoryCorps, and an explosion of information sources about the lives of celebrities, proclaim our fascination with this genre.

If we think of autobiography as informational reading, we're overlooking something important. Nonfiction is often read for the same reasons and pleasures that we read fiction: for entertainment, enlightenment, insight and understanding; or to experience drama, comedy and tragedy. And the most popular nonfiction has a personal aspect to it. Popular histories focus on the role of the individual, self-help books reveal the struggles of the author, and true crime is perennially popular. Nowadays, even cookbooks are filled with personal stories about the cook and her family.

Life stories are personal by definition. But they're more. They're literary. The life stories in this book were all consciously shaped the way a novel is shaped, with a beginning, full of exposition and character development; a middle, often with climactic events; and an ending that ties up what came before with a satisfying resolution. We know that in fiction, the writer has used memory, experience, imagination, and all the tools of creative writing. What we forget, is that life stories are also shaped by these same literary devices.

Definitions

This book uses the term *life stories* to mean books that fall into the categories of memoir and autobiography. We generally think of autobiographies as works that cover a long portion of a person's life, that is, from childhood to old age. The authors are often well-known and their autobiographies cover a lifetime of experience. They are usually reflective and feature a significant level of detail. For example, *Madam Secretary,* former diplomat Madeleine Albright's reflections on her life and long career in politics, would be considered autobiography. The *Autobiography of Malcolm X* and Arthur Miller's *Timebends: A Life* are other examples. A memoir, on the other hand, covers some memorable or meaningful portion of the author's life, often in the context of the times. A wonderful example is *My Life in France,* Julia Child's book about living in France from 1948 to 1954. In it, we learn not only about her introduction to French cooking, but what life was like in France following World War II. Other examples of memoirs are Tobias Wolff's *This Boy's Life* and Lidia Minatoya's *Talking to High Monks in the Snow.* While many famous people have written autobiographies, many memoirs today are written by people who become well-known for writing a memoir.

The Appeal of Life Stories

When Jill Ker Conway, memoirist and author of *When Memory Speaks,* said "why is autobiography the most popular form of fiction for modern readers?" she couldn't have made it clearer: life stories appeal to us in the same way that novels do.[1] Fascinating characters, riveting stories, interesting settings, expressive writing, and distinctive moods are all found in abundance in life stories.

We've all had the experience of reading a novel where we couldn't shake off the conviction that the characters were real. Life stories give us that same feeling of personal connection. We're caught up in the narrator's point of view—we want to see how this life unfolds and what it says to us about our own life. Sometimes it dredges up emotions and memories. We might recognize ourselves in the author's struggle to achieve independence and self-knowledge. Life stories like *She's Not There: A Life in Two Genders* by Jennifer Finney Boylan or *Half the Way Home* by Adam Hochschild match the experience we have in character-driven fiction of feeling that we've spent time with real people.

Since the point of writing a memoir is to tell what happened, many life stories have great plots, like the best page-turning fiction. It's a great reading experience to spend time with a fine storyteller. Memoirs like *The Long Walk: A True Story of a Trek to Freedom* by Slavomir Rawicz or *Wild Swans: Three Daughters of China* by Chang Jung are riveting stories. The old adage "Truth is stranger than fiction" applies to some of these books.

Some authors are able to take us right into the settings of their stories, making us see a time or a place. Just as in novels, setting can be so intertwined with story and character that it forever stands out in our memory. *Clapton: The Autobiography,* by Eric Clapton, takes us back to the frenetic, druggy late 20th-century British rock scene. For those who love armchair travel, Helen Thayer's memoir *Walking the Gobi* will be a treat. Memoirs or autobiographies with a strong setting are often rich in detail about the jobs or interests of the author. Ted Conover's memoir *Newjack: Guarding Sing Sing* puts us inside a maximum security prison from a prison guard's point of view.

In language too, readers can find life stories to suit all types of reading interests. Stylistically, these life stories are very diverse and that's what makes them exciting. If we're reading for information, we may not care too much about the author's language and style, but when we're reading for pleasure, the author needs to draw us in. We all have a life story to tell; it's the skillful writer who compels us to read it. Diana Abu-Jaber's *The Language of Baklava* may have you reading slowly to savor her wonderful descriptions of the Middle East. Enjoy Gerald Durrell's wonderful descriptions of his time in Corfu in *My Family and Other Animals*.

Some life stories make a strong impression on our mood. The author makes us laugh or feel uneasy, or leaves us with a sense of sadness or tragedy, shaking our heads over the way things turned out. A memoir like Augusten Burroughs's *Running with Scissors* will have readers laughing even as they are horrified by this over-the-top memoir that is by turns hilarious, macabre, edgy, and poignant.

Kate Braestrup's memoir *Here If You Need Me* is inspirational and energizing. In Leslie Garis's *House of Happy Endings* we hang on for a very troubling story of a family spiraling out of control.

Criteria for Selection

Since so many wonderful life stories have been published in the last 20 years, the titles selected were well reviewed, appeared on lists of best books or won awards. Titles with earlier publication dates are acknowledged classics or 20th-century titles of enduring appeal. This latter group includes *The Autobiography of Benjamin Franklin, Life on the Mississippi* by Mark Twain, *Narrative of the Life of Frederick Douglass, Diary of a Young Girl* by Anne Frank, and the *Confessions* of St. Augustine, all of which have been influential in the genre. They are still terrific reading; the passage of time has not diminished their appeal.

Memoirs and Truthfulness

In recent years there have been several well-publicized instances of memoirs that were fraudulent or filled with invention. The press has been full of discussions about publishers' fact-checking responsibilities, speculation about authors' motives, acerbic interviews, hot exchanges of letters-to-the-editor, and so forth.

As a result, many memoirs now have disclaimers stating that the author has reconstructed conversations, changed identities, conflated characters, or otherwise adjusted the narrative. Authors routinely claim that although these changes may have altered the veracity of the actual record, they were made in the spirit of the events and contribute to a better narrative flow. As Marie Brenner wrote in the introduction to her memoir about her relationship with her brother: "This is very much my own version of my life."[2]

We all know that memory is fickle and subject to unconscious (and conscious!) revision as we gain distance from events, especially the events of our childhood. None of this is news. To paraphrase Mark Twain, people tend to remember things whether they happened or not.[3] And of course, writers are free to pick and choose who and what appears in their memoir: marriages and family members have been known to vanish from autobiographies.

For many readers, these controversies provoke speculation: how much of what I'm reading is true? For some readers, truthfulness is all-important; for others, the artful reconstruction of personal experience is satisfying without looking further. We don't want to hold authors to a standard of recollection that would take the creative joy out of life stories. Sit back, relax, turn off that critical faculty, and dip into the books listed here. Life stories are literature and that may be the only truth.

Organization and How to Use This Book

This is a book of annotated reading lists organized with serendipity in mind! Titles are grouped together by their appeal to readers, as described above, not necessarily under subject headings that would appear in a library's catalog. In short, subject matter is not the guiding rule. For example, if you are interested in extreme adventures or accounts of life-endangering experiences, try the list titled Living to Tell the Tale: Near-Death Experiences in the Story chapter. If you enjoy memoirs about growing up in earlier times, in small towns, where people reflect on their childhood with gentle humor, try the Small is Beautiful: Life in Rural America list in the Settings chapter. On the other hand, for those cathartic memoirs of dysfunctional families, try Fractured Families: From Adversity to Insight in the Character chapter or Faultlines: Difficult Family Relationships in the Story chapter. In each list, an arrow points to a benchmark title to start with. There are also indicators for award-winning titles and titles that are suitable for book group discussion.

The index can be useful as well: look up a life story that you've enjoyed and check out other titles on that list. Browsing, just like wandering a library's shelves, will help you find new favorites. The index also has subject headings to help track down books on a particular subject, time period, or place, or find that elusive title that has slipped from your memory. Blank pages at the end of the book offer space to add notes and titles.

There are almost 450 titles in this book—just the tip of a very large and wonderful trove of life stories. In her book about memoir, *I Could Tell You Stories: Sojourns in the Land of Memory,* Patricia Hampl plumbs the allure of life stories: "Maybe a reader's love of memoir is less an intrusive lust for confession than a hankering for the intimacy of this first-person voice, the deeply satisfying sense of being spoken to privately. More than a story, we want a voice speaking softly, urgently, in our ear, which is to say, to our heart."[4]

Symbols Used in Annotations

⇨ Start Here   This is a good first title to read from this list.

📖   This book is suitable for book group discussion.

AW   This book was given one or more of the following awards: Pulitzer Prize, National Book Critics Circle Award, National Book Award; or it has appeared on the ALA Notable Books list.

Notes

1. Jill Ker Conway. *When Memory Speaks: Reflections on Autobiography*. New York: Alfred A. Knopf, 1998, p. 3.
2. Marie Brenner. *Apples and Oranges: My Brother and Me, Lost and Found*. New York: Farrar, Straus, and Giroux, 2008.
3. Mark Twain, *The Autobiography of Mark Twain*.
4. Patricia Hampl. *I Could Tell You Stories: Sojourns in the Land of Memory*. New York: W.W. Norton, 1999, p. 19.

Further Reading

If you'd like to learn more about the genre of life stories, the titles below offer food for thought from several different and often intriguing points of view.

Birkerts, Sven. *The Art of Time in Memoir: Then, Again*. St. Paul, MN: Graywolf Press, 2008.

Conway, Jill Ker. *When Memory Speaks: Reflections on Autobiography*. New York: Alfred A. Knopf, 1998.

Hamilton, Nigel. *Biography: a Brief History*. Cambridge: Harvard Press, 2007.

Hampl, Patricia. *I Could Tell You Stories: Sojourns in the Land of Memory*. New York: W.W. Norton, 1999.

Heilbrun, Carolyn G. *Writing a Woman's Life*. New York: W.W. Norton, 1988.

Miller, Nancy K. *But Enough About Me: Why We Read Other People's Lives*. New York: Columbia Press, 2002.

Smith, Sidonie and Julia Watson. *Reading Autobiography: A Guide for Interpreting Life Narratives.* Minneapolis: University of Minnesota Press, 2001.

Zinsser, William, ed. *Inventing the Truth: The Art and Craft of Memoir.* Revised and expanded 2nd ed. Boston: Houghton Mifflin, 1995.

Zinsser, William, ed. *Writing About Your Life: A Journey into the Past.* New York: Marlowe, 2004.

Chapter One

Character

Everybody needs his memories. They keep the wolf of insignificance from
the door.

Saul Bellow

Some life stories are more deeply personal than others; that's the distinguishing characteristic of the memoirs in this chapter. As the French essayist Montaigne said, "It is not my deeds that I write down, it is myself, my essence." We come away from reading these memoirs feeling that we know the authors and have shared their journeys, heard their vibrant, sometimes heartbreaking voices in our ears. They write about coming-of-age, struggling with family expectations and dysfunction, coping with mental health problems, surviving life-threatening trials, crossing cultural boundaries, and finding love—all compelling and significant tasks in our lives.

These writers often admit they felt compelled to tell their story, that it begged to be released onto the page. They gained insight from writing it down. It was cathartic, helpful in moving on. For that reason, the writer's intent is for the reader to make a personal connection. Consequently, readers are more likely to identify with the author in this type of memoir than in others. And beyond that, reading these life stories helps us see our lives more clearly and reframe our own histories.

Readers who enjoy novels written in the first person or from the main character's point of view, or novels where the characters step off the page, should

1

enjoy these memoirs. The pacing is often leisurely: readers need time to get to know the author and the author needs time to set the stage and draw the reader in. That doesn't mean that these memoirs are not compelling, absorbing reads. The annotations will provide clues to the pacing.

Some of these life stories may not have a strong sense of closure; they are lives in process, just like our own. Many writers have written second and third memoirs, carrying their lives forward in time or going over the same time period from a different perspective. It's clear from the popularity of very personal memoirs that readers enjoy the emotional impact, insights, and reflections they provide.

Beating the Odds: Survivors of Awful Childhoods

It's difficult to understand how these children and teens, deprived of the love and support most of us take for granted, made it to adulthood successfully. Read about how they found the inner resources to survive.

Brown, Cupcake
A Piece of Cake: A Memoir. 2006. Crown Publishers, ISBN 9781400052288, 470p.

When Brown's mother died unexpectedly, the California legal system assigned her and her brother to their father's custody—a man they had never met who only wanted their Social Security checks. He left them with an abusive foster mother and Brown began a pattern of running away, living in the streets, and using sex to earn money for alcohol and drugs. With a spirited, pull-no-punches style, she recounts her long road down and how she eventually pulled her life together.

Fox, Paula
Borrowed Finery: A Memoir. 2001. Henry Holt, ISBN 0805068155, 210p.

Novelist and Newbery Award–winning author Fox had an astonishingly awful childhood—as an infant, she was abandoned by her uncaring, self-absorbed parents at an orphanage. She was raised by a compassionate minister in upstate New York, but periodically her parents would appear, whisk her away, and deposit her with strangers. Fox survived by developing a rich interior life and a forced self-sufficiency. This is a Dickensian tale, recounted without self-pity and with a writer's eye for the telling detail.

Hall, Meredith

Without a Map: A Memoir. 2007. Beacon Press, ISBN 9780807072738, 221p.

In 1965, at 16, Hall became pregnant and was cast out by her family, shunned in her small New Hampshire community, and forced to give up her baby. For 10 years she wandered in the United States and Europe, rootless, mourning the loss. After 21 years, the son she gave up found her. Hall explores the painful territory of betrayal and loss and the unspeakable things that family members do to each other in the name of propriety.

Lauck, Jennifer

Blackbird: A Childhood Lost and Found. 2000. Pocket Books, ISBN 0671042556, 406p.

Lauck's beautiful mother made her feel special; her death when Lauck was five tore her world apart. Her father moved Lauck in with his girlfriend Deb, who treated her like a servant. When her father died a few years later, Deb kept her on for the Social Security payments and sent her to work as a maid at a church. Lauck tells her story as she lived it, not as an adult looking back; the immediacy is heartrending and we rejoice at her ultimate rescue. Lauck penned a second memoir titled *Still Waters.*

McGahern, John

All Will Be Well. 2006. Alfred A. Knopf, ISBN 1400044960, 289p. ▢.

McGahern paints a vivid picture of life in rural Ireland in the middle decades of the 20th century. He was very close to his mother, an elementary school teacher who died when he was nine, leaving him and his six siblings at the mercy of their vain and brutal father, a sergeant in the Irish Guards. Despite his hellish childhood, McGahern's love of the Irish countryside infuses this sad memoir with a wonderful lyricism.

Rhodes, Richard

A Hole in the World: An American Boyhood. 2000 (1990). University Press of Kansas, ISBN 0700610383, 283p.

Rhodes's mother committed suicide when he was an infant; later his father married a woman so abusive that he would have been starved or beaten to death if his older brother hadn't gone to the police. Placed in a nurturing private boys' home, they began the long process of healing. Rhodes's account is painful to read but not vindictive, a sad and clear-eyed memoir of a ghastly childhood.

Scheeres, Julia
⇨ *Jesus Land: A Memoir.* 2005. Counterpoint, ISBN 9781582433387, 356p.

Scheeres grew up with two adopted black brothers in 1970s rural Indiana with parents whose fundamentalist religious beliefs papered over abuse and neglect. Scheeres's sense of family came from her bond with brother David; when he was sent to a Christian reform school in the Dominican Republic, she chose to join him. The racism, beatings, attempted rape, and hypocrisy they endured are all recounted by Scheeres with remarkable frankness and a sad, wistful longing for what could have been.

Behind the Scenes: Celebrities' Lives

The grass may look greener for the famous and successful; their life stories often tell us otherwise. You've seen them on the stage, screen, and playing field; now find out about the roots of their ambition and the source of their hard-won, sometimes bittersweet success.

Andrews, Julie
⇨ *Home: A Memoir of My Early Years.* 2008. Hyperion, ISBN 9780786865659, 339p.

Andrews's English childhood was lonely and scary: her parents divorced and she lived through the World War II London bombings with her mother and truculent, alcoholic stepfather in a series of shabby rooms. At age nine she began a grueling round of voice classes and performances; by her teenage years, she was supporting her family. She writes of her rise to stardom in *My Fair Lady* with the warmth, sincerity, and lack of pretension she has always projected on stage and screen.

Armstrong, Lance, with Sally Jenkins
It's Not About the Bike: My Journey Back to Life. 2000. Putnam, ISBN 0399146113, 275p.

Cancer and the Tour de France, deathly illness and incredible strength define Armstrong's life journey. Diagnosed with testicular cancer at age 25 and given only a 50-50 chance of survival, he went on to win international championships and become a father. Armstrong's plainspoken story is filled with the emotional highs and lows of a very full life.

Ashe, Arthur, with Arnold Rampersad
Days of Grace: A Memoir. 1993. Alfred A. Knopf, ISBN 0679423966, 317p.

Ashe broke the color barrier in tennis, captured the hearts of fans, won several Grand Slam championships, and led the U.S. Davis Cup team. His life was complicated by heart disease and AIDS contracted from transfusions during surgery, and he died, too young, at age 50. His moving memoir, completed shortly before his death, reminds us of his personal courage and the depths of his commitment to social justice.

Baronova, Irina
Irina: Ballet, Life and Love. 2006. University Press of Florida, ISBN 0813030269, 544p.

Dance fans will relish Baronova's gracious, star-studded memoir of her life through age 48. She fled the Russian Revolution and studied ballet in Paris; George Balanchine discovered her and she became one of the "Three Baby Ballerinas" who electrified audiences at the Ballet Russe de Monte Carlo. She recounts her tumultuous, passionate life as a dancer and an actress is in a warm, personal style, directly addressing the reader.

Curtis, Tony, with Peter Golenbock
American Prince: A Memoir. 2008. Harmony Books, ISBN 9780307408495, 364p.

In 1948, at the age of 22, Bernie Schwartz walked through the casting door at Universal Studios and signed a seven-year contract. Far from his poverty-stricken childhood on the streets of New York, he became the sultry Tony Curtis, dating Marilyn Monroe and hanging out with Frank Sinatra's Rat Pack. Curtis fills his memoir with inside stories about films and friends, love affairs and marriages, ever grateful that he lived the life of his dreams.

Douglas, Kirk
The Ragman's Son: An Autobiography. 1988. Simon & Schuster, ISBN 0671637177, 510p.

One of the most famous of Hollywood's leading men, Douglas grew up as Issur Danielovitch, dirt poor in upstate New York, the only boy in a family of six girls. He reveals how the anger stored up during a childhood of trying to please a distant and domineering father fueled his acting career.

Hamill, Dorothy, as told to Deborah Amelon
A Skating Life: My Story. 2007. Hyperion, ISBN 9781401303280, 238p.

From our view in the stands, Hamill's life glowed with success: numerous skating championships, an Olympic Gold Medal in 1976, headliner in the Ice Capades. Despite her professional successes and the brilliant smile she always wore, she battled serious family problems and mental illness.

Louganis, Greg, with Eric Marcus
Breaking the Surface. 1995. Random House, ISBN 0679437037, 290p.

Louganis, considered the greatest diver of all time, won multiple medals at three Olympic games. Despite his very public career, he was notoriously shy about his private life until this very candid autobiography revealed the pain, triumph, and controversy inextricably mingled in his life. Louganis, the consummate athlete, was an adoptee with an abusive father, a gay man with an abusive lover, an abuser of drugs and alcohol, and ultimately an HIV-positive advocate for gay rights.

Steinhardt, Arnold
Violin Dreams. 2006. Houghton Mifflin, ISBN 9780618368921, 255p.

Virtuoso violinist Steinhardt, first violinist of the Guarnieri String Quartet, sings the joys of a life spent immersed in classical music. At the age of six he heard a recording of the Beethoven Violin Concerto and found his vocation. In this lively memoir, he recounts his rise to success with modesty and warmth. We follow his progress in technique and interpretation, learn about the instrument, famous violinists, and share Steinhardt's pleasure in his profession.

Walters, Barbara
Audition: A Memoir. 2008. Alfred A. Knopf, ISBN 9780307266460, 612p. 📖.

Walters's candid autobiography reveals the insecurities that drove her ambition. Her father made and lost several fortunes in the nightclub business, her older sister was mildly retarded, and Walters's fears that she would need to support her family ultimately proved true. As a producer in the early days of TV news, she learned the skills that would propel her to fame as an interviewer of politicians, royals, and stars. Well-paced and absorbing, this is a great behind-the-scenes story.

Being Different: Introspective Memoirs

These memoirs take us deep into the lives and thoughts of a unique group of sensitive, introspective individuals. Some have faced overwhelming physical, mental, or emotional problems. As with the best character-driven fiction, we feel a strong personal connection with their stories. Their stories also make us think about the experience of being different.

Cohen, Leah Hager
Train Go Sorry: Inside a Deaf World. 1994. Houghton Mifflin, ISBN 0395636256, 296p. AW.

> Cohen is the hearing granddaughter of a deaf immigrant couple and both her parents taught at the Lexington School for the Deaf in New York. As a child, she lived at the School and the deaf students were her companions and surrogate family; she negotiated the deaf and hearing worlds with ease. With Cohen, we enter another culture, mapping its borders and issues from the perspective of her personal experiences and by following several students from the School.

Grealy, Lucy
⇨ *Autobiography of a Face.* 1994. Houghton Mifflin, ISBN 0395657806, 223p. 📖.

> At the age of nine, Grealy had surgery to remove a cancerous growth in her jaw; her disfigured face made her a target for taunts and stares at school and in the street. Radiation, chemotherapy, and multiple surgeries in subsequent years forced her to cope with the isolation and shame of looking ugly, looking different. Grealy's gift is to take us with her on this private and deeply lonely journey as she examines how the value society places on physical beauty affected her life.

Harris, E. Lynn
What Becomes of the Broken Hearted: A Memoir. 2003. Doubleday, ISBN 0385502648, 266p.

> Novelist Harris grew up poor and black in Arkansas with a pervasive feeling that he was different from everyone around him. As a child, he struggled with an abusive stepfather and later with the knowledge that his homosexuality was unacceptable in the 1950s South. His search for love and self-acceptance is heartfelt and inspirational.

Knighton, Ryan
Cockeyed: A Memoir. 2006. Public Affairs, ISBN 9781586483296, 263p.

> When Knighton was in his late teens, a series of driving accidents and near-accidents could no longer be dismissed as lack of attention: his eyesight was fading due to retinitis pigmentosa. For 15 years, as his vision deteriorated,

Knighton moved from darkness to light in his daily life and in his understanding of the blind and sighted worlds. His memoir has remarkable grace and humor, a very satisfying story of self-discovery.

Moore, Judith
Fat Girl: A True Story. 2005. Hudson Street Press, ISBN 1594630097, 196p.

Moore's love/hate relationship with food began in her awful childhood: her father deserted her, her mother beat her. Food became a source of comfort and shame and made her a target of other children. Moore doesn't ask for the reader's pity or sugar-coat the obsessions that drove her life and the resulting memoir has the ring of deeply felt, hard-won truth.

Oxnam, Robert B.
A Fractured Mind: My Life with Multiple Personality Disorder. 2005. Hyperion, ISBN 1401302270, 285p. 📖.

Oxnam was a well-respected Asia scholar but at age 50 he was coping with destructive behaviors, including alcoholism and bulimia. A psychiatrist diagnosed him with multiple personality disorder (MPD) when "Tommy" appeared at a therapy session, the first of 11 "alters" inhabiting Oxnam's inner world. In succeeding years, Oxnam worked on uncovering the abuse at the root of his disorder, integrating the personalities, and returning to a functional life. Despite the extreme nature of MPD, this engaging narrative will have readers thinking about the various aspects of their own personalities and how we unify our disparate voices.

Sebold, Alice
Lucky: A Memoir. 1999. Scribner, ISBN 0684857820, 254p. 📖.

Not a memoir for the faint of heart, Sebold begins by recounting how she was raped during her freshman year at college. This is powerful, graphic stuff; she hits bottom on the first page and takes a long time to come up. Her story of the road to recovery is gripping and memorable, especially notable for the way she examines her relationships with friends, family, and police in the aftermath of the crime.

White, Edmund
My Lives. 2006. Ecco Press, ISBN 0066213975, 356p.

By dividing his memoir into chapters by theme rather than chronologically, novelist and essayist White is able to paint in depth pictures of individuals, times, and places. He grew up in the 1950s, when homosexuality needed to be "cured," he lived through times of furtive sex, embraced the openness after Stonewall, and entered the fraught AIDS era. White's memoir is literate and insightful, but his frankness may be shocking to some readers.

Breaking Free: Overcoming Adversity

These authors tell us about their transformative journeys: how they broke away from confining situations to change the course of their lives. Some were trapped by economics or politics and escaped at great personal risk. For others, parental expectations or cultural constraints were powerful forces.

Dirie, Waris, and Cathleen Miller
Desert Flower: The Extraordinary Journey of a Desert Nomad. 1998. Wm. Morrow, ISBN 0688158234, 228p.

> *Desert Flower* follows Dirie from childhood, when she herded sheep, goats, and camels in Somalia to a life as a supermodel and activist. Dirie underwent female genital mutilation and ran away from home at 13 to escape an arranged marriage. A job at the Somali ambassador's house in London brought her to the attention of a fashion photographer, and her career was launched. Dirie tells a great story with refreshing delight in her good fortune.

Fisher, Antwone Quenton
Finding Fish: A Memoir. 2001. Wm. Morrow, ISBN 0688176992, 339p.

> When Fisher was born, his teenage mother was in jail for murder and had no interest in him. In foster care he was cruelly abused by a couple who knew how to work the child welfare system. His remarkable story of how he survived to become a husband, father, and successful Hollywood screenwriter is a gripping tale of determination and hope. His life story was made into the movie *Antwone Fisher.*

Li, Cunxin
➪ *Mao's Last Dancer.* 2004. Putnam, ISBN 039915096X, 445p.

> Li was one of 6 brothers in a desperately poor rural Chinese family. At age 11, he was picked for Madame Mao's ballet academy in Beijing. His initial dislike of the dance classes gave way to a steely determination to excel and at 18 he was chosen for a cultural exchange program with the Houston Ballet. The story of how he fell in love with America and subsequently defected from China reads like adventure fiction.

Moody, Anne

Coming of Age in Mississippi. 2004 (1968). Delta Trade Paperback, ISBN 0385337817, 424p. 📖.

Moody was raised in a Southern sharecropper's shack in the 1940s and 1950s. A curious and thoughtful child, she saw and deplored the effects of the racism and violence around her. She became a prominent activist in the civil rights movement, focusing on the rights of women and children. Her memoir, which made waves for its originality when it was first published, is compulsively readable for her wonderful characterizations and colloquial tone.

Nafisi, Azar

Reading Lolita in Tehran: A Memoir in Books. 2003. Random House, ISBN 0375504907, 347p. 📖.

From 1995 to 1997, the author courted danger by holding a class in her Tehran home to discuss Western literature with a group of women university students. The books they read and discussed—*Lolita, The Great Gatsby, Pride and Prejudice,* among others—helped them cope with their own restricted lives and find a sense of camaraderie and freedom. Nafisi successfully combines literary criticism and personal stories in this very poignant memoir. A second memoir, *Things I've Been Silent About,* covers her difficult childhood in Iran.

Rodriguez, Richard

Hunger of Memory: The Education of Richard Rodriguez: An Autobiography. 2004 (1982). Bantam Books, ISBN 0553382519, 212p. AW. 📖.

For Rodriguez growing up in Sacramento, California, Spanish was the language that signaled home and safety; Inglés was part of the outside world. Rodriguez learned English to create a public persona and achieve success, but at a great personal cost. In a memoir that grapples meticulously with the question of how language relates to identity, he tells how fluency in English changed his relationship to his family and culture.

Thomas, Piri

Down These Mean Streets. 1997 (1967). Vintage Books ISBN 0679781420, 340p. AW. 📖.

Thomas grew up in 1930s Spanish Harlem. A dark-skinned Puerto Rican, struggling with racism, poverty, and the anger of the marginalized, he was drawn into a self-destructive life of drugs, gangs, and crime, and served time in prison. His bitter struggle to come to terms with his racial and ethnic identity is written with a no-holds-barred fidelity that has made his memoir a classic for 40 years.

Wong, Jade Snow
 Fifth Chinese Daughter. 1989 (1950). University of Washington Press, ISBN
  0295968265, 246p.

   Wong was raised in San Francisco's Chinatown in the 1930s, the daughter
   of very traditional parents. She writes in the third person, from a child's perspective, about how her world was constricted by her parents' expectations for
   her to be a good Chinese daughter. Wong was determined that her life would
   be different; how she gained an education and career in the face of their op-
   position makes a moving and delightful tale.

Caught in the Crossfire: People in Danger

If your life has been smooth sailing, try these memoirs written by people
who grew up in dangerous times and places. They survived, often at great cost,
and their moving memoirs enrich our understanding of courage in the face of
adversity.

Appleman-Jurman, Alicia
 Alicia: My Story. 1988. Bantam Books, ISBN 0553053175, 356p. 📖.

   Alicia was only nine years old when World War II began, and although
   she managed to elude death at the hands of Communists and Nazis, she lost her
   entire family. With incredible courage and nerve, she not only survived but ran
   a Jewish orphanage and led secret transports to Palestine. An inspiring story
   related with heart pounding immediacy.

Arenas, Reinaldo, trans. by Dolores M. Koch
 Before Night Falls. 1993. Viking Press, ISBN 0670840785, 317p. AW.

   Arenas grew up with his mother's family in a poor, rural part of Cuba; in
   his teens he joined the rebels fighting against Batista, but grew disillusioned
   with Castro's repressive policies. Under Castro, he was persecuted for his homosexuality and his writing, even as his translated novels were acclaimed in
   Europe. His memoir is a powerful statement of personal and political belief,
   completed shortly before his death from AIDS in New York City.

Cooper, Helene
 ⇨ *The House at Sugar Beach: In Search of a Lost African Childhood.* 2008.
  Simon & Schuster, ISBN 9780743266246, 352p.

   Cooper's ancestors were the free American blacks who settled Liberia in
   1820; she grew up as part of an elite governing class, in a luxurious 22-room

beach house. A coup in 1980 changed all that and her family fled to America, leaving her adopted sister Eunice behind to cope with the ensuing corruption and violence. After years traveling around the world as a journalist, Cooper returned to Liberia to find her sister and make amends for her family's betrayal.

Hari, Daoud, as told to Dennis Michael Burke and Megan McKenna

The Translator: A Tribesman's Memoir of Darfur. 2008. Random House, ISBN 9781400067442, 204p.

Hari saw his childhood village destroyed with horrific brutality by the Sudanese army and government-sponsored militias. He felt compelled to give a voice to the victims of this terrible genocide and worked as a translator, risking his life to take journalists into the danger zones. Hari's humanity and compassion shine through in this lucid and revealing account of how senseless violence destroyed a beautiful ancient culture.

Hayslip, Le Ly, with Jay Wurts

When Heaven and Earth Changed Places: A Vietnamese Woman's Journey from War to Peace. 1989. Plume, ISBN 0452264170, 368p.

As a Vietnamese peasant and teenager during the Vietnam War, Hayslip lived in a nightmarish world where she did whatever she could to survive, even if it was illegal or dangerous. She was at times a Viet Cong courier, a black marketeer, a hospital worker, and a prostitute, none of which saved her from torture, rape, and harassment by both sides in the conflict. Fortunately, this moving tale of courage and the horrific effects of war on civilians closes with a happy ending. In the sequel, *Child of War, Woman of Peace,* she writes about her turbulent life in Southern California, where she was twice widowed and raised two sons.

Min, Anchee

Red Azalea. 1994. Pantheon, ISBN 067942332X, 306p. 📖.

A quietly devastating tale of a young woman's life in China during the Cultural Revolution. Min was a Little Red Guard leader at school and was forced to denounce a favorite teacher; later she was sent to a work farm where she spent years in forced labor. In this lonely, regimented existence, she took comfort from a forbidden love with her female squad leader. Min's unsentimental account is both heart wrenching and thought provoking.

Nemat, Marina

Prisoner of Tehran: A Memoir. 2007. Free Press, ISBN 9781416537427, 306p.

Nemat was only 16 when she was arrested, imprisoned in Tehran's infamous Evin Prison, tortured, and condemned to death. A guard offered to save her life if she married him and converted to Islam from Christianity. Nemat's strong sense of justice and compassion helped her through this terrifying time. She alternates the account of her prison experiences with chapters about her early life and the violent changes the fundamentalist regime brought to Iran.

Oufkir, Malika, and Michelle Fitoussi, trans. by Ros Schwartz
 Stolen Lives: Twenty Years in a Desert Jail. 2001. Talk Miramax Books, ISBN 0786867329, 293p. 📖.
   Oufkir was adopted by the King of Morocco as a playmate for his daughter and grew up alongside her in the luxurious palace. In 1972, her father was murdered for his part in a coup; for 20 years she was imprisoned with her mother and siblings in a series of remote prisons, in harsh conditions, often isolated from one another. Oufkir tells a harrowing tale of how they endured and the bittersweet experience of their ultimate return to freedom. Readers may also enjoy her follow-up memoir, *Freedom: The Story of My Second Life.*

Satrapi, Marjane
 Persepolis. 2003. Pantheon, ISBN 0375422307, 153p. 📖.
   When Satrapi was 10, the Shah of Iran was overthrown; her family welcomed the new regime, only to find that its repressive fundamentalist religious policies put them and their liberal relatives at risk. In a graphic narrative that is all the more poignant for its black-and-white understated drawings, Satrapi charts her life as a rebellious, frightened teen, as she sees the home and family she loved swept away. The memoir was made into a film of the same title. A sequel, *Persepolis 2,* follows Satrapi into adulthood.

Crossing Borders: Making a Life in a New Country

There are both positive and negative emotional and psychological experiences involved in moving to another country. These writers share with us their disorientation and sense of loss. Some ached with longing for language, culture, food, and family. Others welcomed the chance to become immersed in another culture and see the world through different eyes.

Ansary, Tamim
 West of Kabul, East of New York: An Afghan American Story. 2002. Farrar, Straus and Giroux, ISBN 0374287570, 292p.
   After September 11, 2001, Ansary, who grew up in Afghanistan and the United States, sent an e-mail to a few friends hoping that his perspective could

counter the hatred expressed toward Afghanistan and Islam in the media. His e-mail spread around the world; the response helped Ansary understand that his own story, which embodied the conflict between East and West, could bring understanding and reconciliation.

Arana, Marie

⇨ *American Chica: Two Worlds, One Childhood.* 2001. Dial Press, ISBN 0385319622, 309p. AW.

Recalling her childhood as the daughter of a Peruvian father and an American mother, Arana tells how these competing cultures complicated and enriched her life. In Peru, she was taught to be a lady; on the Wyoming ranch of her mother's family she learned how to shoot a gun and ride a horse. In rich and loving detail, she limns these contrasting cultures and how they clashed in her family life. Readers may also enjoy her novel *Cellophane,* set on a hacienda in the rainforest and filled with the vivid colors and textures of the Amazon jungle.

Hoffman, Eva

Lost in Translation: A Life in a New Language. 1989. E.P. Dutton, ISBN 0525246010, 280p. 📖.

Hoffman's Holocaust survivor parents remained in Poland after World War II but continuing anti-Semitism made their lives difficult and dangerous. In 1959, when Hoffman was 13, they immigrated to Vancouver, Canada. This is the story of Hoffman's efforts to make a place for herself in America as the daughter of survivors and as an exile from her beloved Cracow. She writes achingly of the difficulties of learning to express herself in a new language.

Santiago, Esmeralda

When I Was Puerto Rican. 1994. Vintage Books, ISBN 0679756760, 274p.

Santiago grew up in a tin shack in a rural Puerto Rican barrio, the oldest of seven children with a philandering and often absent father. She describes a difficult but vibrant world, full of friends and relatives joyously celebrating life. Her move to Brooklyn as a young teenager thrust her into a drab, cold world, but fired her with ambition to use education as a way out. She continued the story of her life in Brooklyn in the 1960s in *Almost a Woman.*

Shepard, Sadia

The Girl from Foreign: A Search for Shipwrecked Ancestors, Forgotten Histories, and a Sense of Home. 2008. Penguin Press, ISBN 9781594201516, 364p.

Growing up in a diverse and accepting household—her father was a white Presbyterian and her mother a Pakistani Muslim—Shepard was stunned to learn that her beloved Muslim grandmother was actually born to a Jewish family in Bombay, part of the Bene Israel who came to India two thousand years ago. Her compelling memoir about her trip to India to understand this unexpected part of her heritage alternates with chapters about her mother's family history.

Swiller, Josh

The Unheard: A Memoir of Deafness and Africa. 2007. Henry Holt, ISBN 9780805082104, 265p. 📖.

Mostly deaf from birth, Swiller's hearing aids and lip-reading helped, but he always felt like an outsider, on the fringes of the hearing world. When he joined the Peace Corps, he hoped that he could find "a place past deafness and hearing." In his assigned Zambian village he earnestly set about trying to make a difference, but came up against a culture of violence with profound consequences for the villagers, his friends, and his own future. This story reads easily, but has a powerful impact.

Turnbull, Sarah

Almost French: A New Life in Paris. 2002. Bantam Books, ISBN 1863252851, 309p. 📖.

On holiday, journalist Turnbull meets Frederic, an attractive lawyer, who invites her to visit him in Paris, where their romance blossoms and she sets about adjusting to her new home. She quickly learns that her informal Aussie style of dress, drinking, and socializing raises eyebrows among Frederic's friends; she has entered a culture with its own rules and expectations. Her memoir of how she learned the hard way to (almost) fit in is filled with humor and rueful observations about how she came to love her new life in France.

Yang, Kao Kalia

The Latehomecomer: A Hmong Family Memoir. 2008. Coffee House, ISBN 9781566892087, 277p.

The Hmong, an ethnic minority living in Laos, aided the CIA during the Vietnam War; afterwards they were hunted down by the Pathet Lao and North Vietnamese. Yang's family escaped to Thailand where she was born in a refugee camp in 1980. With richly detailed and haunting descriptions, she contrasts her early childhood in the camps, poor in material things but rich in family, with her life in Minnesota, where the loss of language, culture, and beloved grandmother left her lonely and silent.

Extraordinary Women's Lives

Like exciting novels, these provocative, inspirational life stories are filled with conflict and turmoil in the lives of women who blazed new trails, pushed societal limits, and sometimes changed the world in the process.

Antin, Mary
The Promised Land. 2001 (1912). Modern Library, ISBN 0375757392, 328p.

Antin arrived in Boston at the age of 14 from a Russian village. Although she lived in the poorest of slums, ambition and thirst for education enabled her to transcend her surroundings, meet and correspond with well-known intellectuals of her day, and attend Columbia Teachers College. This is the quintessential American immigrant story, told with verve and lyrical idealism. *The Promised Land* has been continuously in print since its 1912 publication.

Betancourt, Ingrid, trans. by Steve Rendall
Until Death Do Us Part: My Struggle to Reclaim Colombia. 2002. Ecco Press, ISBN 0060008903, 228p.

Betancourt's parents were deeply involved in Colombian politics and diplomacy; despite her privileged French childhood, she felt the same commitment to her country and returned to become a legislator. Her fight against corruption and the drug cartels brought death threats, smear campaigns, and isolation from family. Her fast-paced memoir reads like a political thriller; after it was published, she was kidnapped and held hostage in the Colombian jungle for six and a half years.

Conway, Jill Ker
⇨ *The Road from Coorain.* 1989. Alfred A. Knopf, ISBN 0394574567, 238p. AW. 📖.

Conway spent her early childhood on a 30,000 acre sheep ranch in the Australian outback, homeschooled and free-spirited. When she was 11, after the death of her father and older brother, the family moved to Sydney, where her mother suffered from alcoholism and depression. Conway's struggle to find her own way to independent adulthood has become a classic of women's memoirs. She writes about her life in the United States and Canada—education, career, and marriage—in a second volume of autobiography, *True North.*

Cook, Ida

Safe Passage: The Remarkable True Story of Two Sisters Who Rescued Jews from the Nazis. 2008. Harlequin, ISBN 9780373892013, 286p.

Cook and her sister Louise came of age in 1920s London, two women of singular integrity and character. Avid opera fans, they scrimped to afford trips outside England to hear their favorite singers, like Galli-Curci and Pinza. When they traveled to Germany in the 1930s, their opera friends opened their eyes to Hitler's persecution of the Jews. Unable to stand by, the sisters rescued dozens of Jews, arranging safe passage for them to England. Ida's matter-of-fact attitude toward their dangerous work is a tribute to the sisters' moral courage.

Cox, Lynne

Swimming to Antarctica: Tales of a Long-Distance Swimmer. 2004. Alfred A. Knopf, ISBN 0375415076, 323p.

From childhood, Lynne loved swimming long distances, learning how to conserve body heat and husband her strength. At 14, she swam across the 26-mile Catalina Channel and then the English Channel, setting a new record. Other remarkable swims followed, all over the world. She endured physical difficulties, harsh conditions, and encounters with sharks, always challenging herself in this inspirational story of endurance and determination.

Graham, Katherine

Personal History. 1997. Alfred A. Knopf, ISBN 0394585852, 642p. AW. 📖.

We know Graham as the feisty owner of the *Washington Post* newspaper who approved the publication of the Pentagon Papers, but her memoir tells a very personal story of struggle and success. Her manic-depressive, charismatic husband Phil Graham was the *Post*'s owner; Katherine was always in his shadow, as she had been with her parents. It was only when Phil committed suicide in 1963 that her remarkable career began.

Keller, Helen

The Story of My Life: The Restored Edition. 2005 (1903). Pocket Books, ISBN 1416500324, 282p.

Keller was born in 1880 and became deaf and blind from a fever at 19 months. Just before she turned seven, her parents hired Anne Sullivan to tutor her. The famous story of the moment when Keller understood the manual alphabet and broke out of her isolation is still inspirational. The story of Keller's triumph over her disabilities, her drive to learn and explore the world, and Sullivan's devotion to her student, is too good to miss.

Piercy, Marge

Sleeping with Cats: A Memoir. 2002. Wm. Morrow, ISBN 0066211158, 345p.

> Piercy grew up in a working-class family in Detroit in the 1930s and 1940s. Her turbulent childhood included membership in a gang and struggles with her volatile father. Smart in an era that devalued women's intelligence, politically and sexually active when women were expected to be neither, she was always at odds with traditional women's roles. The strength of this memoir lies in Piercy's evocation of her emotional life, with special note of her many beloved cats. Piercy's novels, many with a feminist slant, have a devoted readership: *Small Changes, Gone to Soldiers, Woman on the Edge of Time,* among others.

Fathers and Sons

As far back as ancient times, literature is filled with stories of father-son relationships fraught with competition, secrets, expectations, and abuse. It's a powerful theme, as these memoirs prove. The accounts vary in tone from intense to humorous, and we meet some very unusual fathers and sons.

Ackerley, J. R. (Joe Randolph)

My Father & Myself. 1999 (1969.) New York Review Books, ISBN 0940322129, 283p.

> The startling opening sentence of this classic memoir sets the stage for further revelations about Ackerley's eccentric and secretive father. "The Banana King," as his father was known, was an authoritative, distant presence; not until after his death was Ackerley to understand the reasons. As he tells the full story, Ackerley also reveals, with remarkable wit and candor, his own experiences as a homosexual.

Burnside, John

A Lie About My Father. 2007. Graywolf Press, ISBN 9781555974671, 277p. 📖.

> Burnside grew up in Scotland and England, in sad, lonely industrial towns, where he and his mother and sister were dominated by a tyrannical father whose drunken rages, lies, and deceits kept any trace of joy or comfort from their lives. The unbearable tension in the family relationships drove Burnside to take refuge in books and imaginative fantasies, but also to drugs and delinquency, leaving him with an abiding sense of worthlessness. With a poet's elegance and lucidity, he draws us into the dark vortex of his youth and struggle to escape.

Coates, Ta-Nehisi

The Beautiful Struggle: A Father, Two Sons and an Unlikely Road to Manhood. 2008. Spiegel & Grau, ISBN 9780385520362, 223p.

Coates grew up in violent 1980s Baltimore, a time when young African American men killed each other over "sneakers stitched by serfs." His father, Paul Coates, a former Black Panther leader and founder of Black Classic Press, had strong feelings about how his sons should live their lives. Coates was bookish and introverted; he tells the layered story of his difficult childhood in rhythmic, street-smart prose.

Gilmour, David

The Film Club. 2008. Twelve, ISBN 9780446199292, 225p. 📖.

Gilmour allowed his disaffected 15-year-old son, Jesse, to drop out of high school if he agreed to watch three movies every week with his father. They spent several years watching and talking about films—from *The Four Hundred Blows* to *Pulp Fiction*—and in the process father and son learned about each other and connected in unexpected ways.

Hochschild, Adam

⇨ *Half the Way Home: A Memoir of Father and Son.* 2005 (1986). Houghton Mifflin, ISBN 061843920X, 197p. AW. 📖.

Hochschild's gripping psychological study of his relationship with his father takes us deep into the life of a wealthy, privileged family, especially during summers at Eagle Nest, their beautiful Adirondack compound. Hochschild's father was distant and demanding, raining down humiliating lectures for behavioral infractions his son could hardly comprehend. In adulthood, Hochschild finally gained the distance to understand the family dynamics and accept the very different life he had chosen.

Morris, Bob

Assisted Loving: True Tales of Double Dating with My Dad. 2008. HarperCollins, ISBN 9780061374128, 288p.

After his wife's death, Morris's 80-year-old father Joe began to date and enlisted his son to vet the personal ads for him. Morris, a gay journalist, was also cruising the personals, hoping for a lasting relationship, but he was too judgmental about his dates and hypercritical of his "irritating, never dull" father. This is a funny and tender story of how they both learn that we're never too old for love, parental or romantic: we just have to let it find us.

Nuland, Sherwin

Lost in America: A Journey with My Father. 2003. Alfred A. Knopf, ISBN 0375412948, 209p. 📖.

A well-known surgeon and author, Nuland writes about his childhood, which was dominated by his father Meyer, a bitter, ailing man with an explosive temper, whose forceful personality overshadowed Nuland's life and caused Nuland crippling episodes of depression. Nuland's candid story is painful and raw, a grim, claustrophobic tale about what happens when love is withheld. Readers may also enjoy his insightful books about medicine: *How We Die* and *How We Live* (originally titled *The Wisdom of the Body*).

Sheff, David

Beautiful Boy: A Father's Journey through His Son's Meth Addiction. 2006. Houghton Mifflin, ISBN 9780618683352, 326p. 📖.

Instantly engrossing, Sheff's heartbreaking story of his son Nic's meth addiction is filled with the anguish of a parent who wants to know where it all went wrong. Torn between blame and guilt, Sheff searches his life and relationship with Nic: his own youthful drug-taking, the divorce that sent Nic shuttling between San Francisco and Los Angeles, his remarriage, and Nic's school experiences. It's a unique but universal story of a parent's love and desperate heartache. For an interesting perspective, read Nic's own memoir, called *Tweak: Growing Up on Methamphetamines.*

Wolff, Geoffrey

The Duke of Deception: Memories of My Father. 1990 (1979). Vintage Books, ISBN 0679727523, 275p.

Wolff's father Arthur, self-styled "Duke," was a flamboyant, charismatic con artist who faked an Ivy League résumé and left a trail of debt and crime in his peripatetic wake. Wolff lived with his father after his parents divorced and although he never doubted his father's love, he was ultimately a victim of his desperate scams. Wolff's brother, Tobias, who lived with their mother, wrote of his own struggles in the memoir *This Boy's Life.*

Fractured Families: From Adversity to Insight

Family: we may not be able to live with them, but we can rarely write memoirs without them. These authors tell very personal stories of how they struggled in difficult, dysfunctional family situations.

Anderson, Walter
  Meant to Be: The True Story of a Son Who Discovers He Is His Mother's Deepest Secret. 2003. HarperCollins, ISBN 0060099062, 243p.

Anderson had a strong sense that he was different from his siblings and schoolmates, certainly different from the volatile father who beat him throughout his childhood. Filled with anger and confusion, he dropped out of high school and joined the Marines; on leave to attend his father's funeral, he learned the truth of his origins and embarked on a voyage of self-discovery in this tense, page-turning memoir.

Dawidoff, Nicholas
  The Crowd Sounds Happy: A Story of Love, Madness, and Baseball. 2008. Pantheon, ISBN 9780375400285, 271p. 📖.

Baseball helped Dawidoff navigate a rocky childhood after his parents' divorce when he felt that his life was off-kilter. His mother struggled with the responsibility for two children and never explained the reasons for his father's frightening behavior. In a memoir that manages to be simultaneously luminous and disconcerting, Dawidoff describes how devotion to the Red Sox and playing baseball helped ease the pain of growing up different.

Gallagher, Tim
  Falcon Fever: A Falconer in the Twenty-First Century. 2008. Houghton Mifflin, ISBN 9780618805754, 326p.

Gallagher discovered falconry at age 12 and was hooked on training and flying the beautiful birds; it was a distraction from an unhappy home life. Through falconry he found friends—some also struggling with demons—and fell into a life of petty crime before landing on his feet. In midlife, he traveled to sites in Europe associated with the great falconer Emperor Frederick II; this reconnection with falconry helped him find a sense of peace in a fragmented life.

Hamill, Pete
  ⇨ *A Drinking Life: A Memoir.* 1994. Little, Brown and Co., ISBN 0316341088, 265p. 📖.

Journalist Hamill draws us into his childhood world of Brooklyn in the 1940s and 1950s, where his father was a demanding and boozy presence and life was lived most fully on the streets. Drinking seemed to be what adult life was about and it provided an escape for Hamill too by the time he was in high school. He is frank about the rewards and punishments of drink and unapologetic about the way it ruined his marriage. He calls his memoir "the tale that has no hero" but his insights will keep readers turning pages. Hamill's fiction, set in New York, has a strong sense of place; readers may enjoy *Snow in August* or *North River.*

Nafisi, Azar
Things I've Been Silent About: Memories. 2008. Random House, ISBN 9781400063611, 336p. ⬚.

This companion to Nafisi's memoir *Reading Lolita in Tehran* tells her personal story of growing up in a difficult household where she was caught between her cold, demanding mother and her literary, adulterous father. The years of political turbulence in Iran also affected their lives: her father, once Tehran's mayor, spent time in jail and her mother served a term in Parliament. Nafisi's story of how she married young to escape from her mother and how she found her own voice in America is remarkable for its insight.

Pearson, Felicia "Snoop," and David Ritz
Grace After Midnight: A Memoir. 2007. Grand Central Publishing, ISBN 9780446195188, 233p.

Pearson—"Snoop" on the HBO series *The Wire*—tells how despite growing up in a loving and stable foster family, she gravitated to a life of crime on the Baltimore streets, dealing drugs and serving time for murder. Her street-smart voice tells how it all went down, in a punchy, rhythmic, slangy style.

Roiphe, Anne Richardson
1185 Park Avenue. 1999. Free Press, ISBN 0684857316, 257p. ⬚.

This memoir is proof that wealth is no guarantee of happiness. Roiphe grew up on the fashionable Upper East Side of Manhattan in the 1940s and 1950s, part of a family that was rich in material things, but spiritually impoverished. Her unhappily married parents were self-absorbed and emotionally unavailable. With bitterness and a razor-sharp eye for detail, Roiphe charts how she navigated the minefields of her childhood. A later memoir, *Epilogue,* is a graceful account of adjusting to widowhood.

Trussoni, Danielle
Falling Through the Earth: A Memoir. 2006. Henry Holt, ISBN 9780805077322, 240p.

Some Vietnam veterans came home with wounds that couldn't be healed: Trussoni's swaggering, charismatic father was scarred by his years as a tunnel rat in Vietnam. When her mother threw him out, Trussoni went too and spent years sitting next to him at his favorite bar as he became drunk and violent. With an unsparing eye and remarkable descriptive powers, she recounts how she traveled to Vietnam to understand the roots and legacies of that time.

Identity Papers: Discovering Our True Selves

One of the basic tasks of growing up is establishing our identity. We all need to do the hard work of separating from our families and setting our own course in life. These authors write about doing just that as they worked through issues of race, gender, and ethnicity, to come to terms with who they are.

Boylan, Jennifer Finney
⇨ *She's Not There: A Life in Two Genders.* 2003. Broadway Books, ISBN 076791404X, 300p. 📖.

From early childhood, Boylan knew he was a girl trapped in a boy's body; in his early 40s, a tenured professor, already married with children, he finally became Jennifer, risking everything he knew and loved to be the person he was always meant to be. With the skills of a fine novelist, Boylan makes the pain and joy of his journey vivid and compelling. In his second memoir, *I'm Looking Through You: Growing Up Haunted,* he writes about his childhood.

Fong-Torres, Ben
Rice Room: Growing Up Chinese-American—from Number Two Son to Rock 'n' Roll. 1994. Hyperion, ISBN 0060099062, 260p.

Fong-Torres fondly remembers the contrast in his childhood between the "rice room" in his father's restaurant and the outside world of American popular culture. This is a bittersweet tale about how assimilation separates parents and children. Readers who remember—or would like a window into—growing up in San Francisco in the turbulent and heady years of the late 1960s and early 1970s will enjoy this memoir from one of the original editors of *Rolling Stone Magazine.*

Minatoya, Lidia
Talking to High Monks in the Snow. 1992. HarperCollins, ISBN 0060168099, 269p. AW. 📖.

Growing up in upstate New York and hearing her parents' stories about Japanese family and culture, Minatoya was caught between two cultures, never quite comfortable in either. It was only after she spent an extended time in

Japan, visiting family members and traveling around the country, that she began to understand who she was and where she belonged.

Nissel, Angela
Mixed: My Life in Black and White. 2006. Villard, ISBN 9780345481146, 228p.

Nissel grew up in West Philadelphia in the 1970s and 1980s with a mixed race heritage—her father was white and her mother African American—navigating between two communities, never quite understanding how to behave in either one. Although her story is laugh-out-loud funny, the pain and awkwardness of her childhood are always evident.

Obama, Barack
Dreams from My Father: A Story of Race and Inheritance. 2007 (1995). Crown Publishers, ISBN 9780307383419, 442p. 📖.

Obama's conversational, eloquent, and very candid autobiography is filled with his thoughts on how race, parentage, and economics have shaped his life. The son of a white American mother and a black Kenyan father he never knew, he grew up in Hawaii with his mother's family. After his father died, he visited the sources of both sides of his family, Kansas and Kenya, in an attempt to understand the nature of his dual heritage.

Smith, Bob
Hamlet's Dresser: A Memoir. 2002. Scribner, ISBN 0684852691, 287p.

Smith's childhood was forever changed when his sister Carolyn was born severely retarded and an unthinking relative blamed him. With his distant father and devastated mother, he lived in an eerie, claustrophobic world. At age 10, reading Shakespeare's words, he found comfort, healing, and a vocation. In Smith's painful, touching account, he makes us feel the extraordinary power of literature to change lives.

Stavans, Ilan
On Borrowed Words: A Memoir of Language. 2001. Viking Press, ISBN 0670877638, 263p.

Stavans's unusual upbringing, in a close-knit, Yiddish-speaking Jewish community in Mexico City, failed to provide him with a sense of identity as a citizen of any country. It took several years of traveling, to the United States, Spain, Israel, and back again to Mexico, for him to find which place he could truly call home. Each chapter in this perceptive memoir focuses on his relationship with a different family member.

Tharps, Lori L.
 Kinky Gazpacho: Life, Love & Spain. 2008. Atria Books, ISBN 9780743296472, 206p.
  As a middle-class African American growing up in Milwaukee suburbs, Tharps was confused about who she was, often brought up short by racial jokes from her white friends, rejected by the black kids as being "too white." She loved all things Spanish and spent a college year in Salamanca, hoping it would be different there for African Americans. The lessons she learned helped her understand who she was and how she would live her life.

Insiders: People Who Made History

Anyone who's dreamed of a life on the front lines of history or discovery will enjoy these accounts, some classic, some from the recent past. They're written by an impressive group of people who have made tremendous contributions in very different fields; their autobiographies are filled with personal details and insight into their lives and times.

Albright, Madeleine Korbel, with Bill Woodward
 Madam Secretary. 2003. Miramax Books, ISBN 0786868430, 562p.
  Albright, the first female secretary of state, combines the personal and professional in this candid glimpse into the world of foreign diplomacy. As a child, she fled Czechoslovakia, belatedly discovering that her parents abandoned Judaism to avoid anti-Semitic persecution; as secretary of state she emphasized the protection of human rights. Her memoir is filled with fascinating insider details about negotiations, world leaders, and conflicts within the White House.

Clinton, Bill
 My Life. 2004. Alfred A. Knopf, ISBN 0375414576, 957p. 📖.
  This is autobiography in the old-fashioned style, combining recollection of events and reflection on their significance. Clinton opens with his childhood in Arkansas, how family and community influenced his character, detailing how his growing interest in politics shaped his choices. Candid and often gripping, filled with the issues and controversies of his presidency and personal life, readers will find an in-depth account of a turbulent era by a major player.

Collins, Michael

Carrying the Fire: An Astronaut's Journey. 2001 (1974). Cooper Square Press, ISBN 081541028X, 478p.

   Collins was overjoyed to be part of the second group of astronauts selected; his first flight was Gemini 10. On July 20, 1969, he orbited in the command module above the moon as Neil Armstrong took the first steps on the lunar surface. His detailed description of his personal journey to that moment is also filled with information about space flight and training and the wonder of seeing our beautiful earth through a rocket window.

Douglass, Frederick

Narrative of the Life of Frederick Douglass, an American Slave, Written by Himself. 2005 (1845). Signet Classics, ISBN 0451529944, 144p.

   Douglass's 1845 account of the brutality and hypocrisy of slavery is a masterpiece of description and insight that speaks directly to the morality of slaveholding. He grew up on a Maryland plantation known for its harsh treatment of slaves; in his teens he was sent to Baltimore where he learned to read and write. From there he escaped to the North and became famous for his work in the Abolitionist movement.

Franklin, Benjamin

The Autobiography of Benjamin Franklin. 2004 (1794). Simon & Schuster, ISBN 0743255062, 143p.

   Franklin began writing his life story for his son in 1771, hoping that he would be interested in his father's life and family history. It is our good fortune that he didn't stop with his family history, but kept writing until 1790, covering the first 51 years of his life. Many of Franklin's accomplishments are known to every schoolchild in the United States, but the sum total of his contributions in politics, science, and education is remarkable, considering that he was self-taught. Told with wit and verve, this is a classic to be savored.

Greenspan, Alan

The Age of Turbulence: Adventures in a New World. 2007. Penguin Press, ISBN 9781594201318, 531p. 📖.

   Former Federal Reserve Board chairman Greenspan looks over his career—personal and public—reflecting on the changes he has seen, the people he has known, and his major role in the economic scene of the past 60 years. Playing jazz was his first love but a talent for statistics led him into the new field of econometrics at an exciting time of sweeping financial changes after World War II. Lucid and engaging, Greenspan's memoir entertains and enlightens.

Mandela, Nelson

➪ *Long Walk to Freedom: The Autobiography of Nelson Mandela.* 1994. Little, Brown and Co., ISBN 0316545856, 558p. 📖.

Mandela's dedication to the eradication of apartheid in South Africa brought him the Nobel Peace Prize, but only after long, terrible years of struggle. His elegant, reflective account starts with his childhood as the foster son of a tribal chieftain. His account continues with his growing awareness of racial oppression and how his underground political activity put his family at risk and led to his trial and incarceration for 27 years, his triumphant return to freedom, and the dismantling of the apartheid regime.

Marching to Their Own Drum: Unique Individuals

These people are visionaries and pioneers and they act on their beliefs. Their lives take unexpected paths for many reasons: intellectual curiosity, physical handicaps, political or moral beliefs, or just plain orneriness. Their wildly different stories are linked by the authors' refusal to do the expected thing. Often, our world is a better place for their efforts.

Friedan, Betty

Life So Far: A Memoir. 2000. Simon & Schuster, ISBN 0684807890, 399p.

From the woman who jumpstarted the feminist revolution, a history of how it all came to be. Friedan's no-nonsense memoir starts with her lonely childhood in Peoria, early literary triumphs at Smith College, stints as a labor reporter, and life as a suburban housewife in the 1950s. Research on women's issues for articles she wrote for *McCall's* and *Ladies Home Journal* opened her eyes to the inequities and frustrations in women's lives. She wrote her breakthrough book, *The Feminist Mystique* in 1963, founded NOW, and led the fight for women's equality.

Gandhi, Mahatma, trans. by Mahadev Desai

An Autobiography: The Story of My Experiments with Truth. 1993 (1957). Beacon Press, ISBN 0807059099, 528p. AW. 📖.

Gandhi was one of the most influential thinkers of the 20th century for his doctrine of nonviolent resistance—*satyagraha*—and for a lifetime of truth seeking and courage. He was born in India in 1869, but lived for many years in South Africa, where his philosophy was developed in response to discrimination against the Indian population. His autobiography is rich in spirituality and humility, providing food for thought for contemplative readers.

Heyerdahl, Thor
Kon-Tiki: Across the Pacific by Raft. 1984 (1953). Rand McNally, ISBN 0528810359, 303p. AW.

Flying in the face of accepted research, Heyerdahl believed Polynesia was settled by people who came from South America, not Southeast Asia. To prove his claim, in 1947 he assembled a crew, built balsa wood rafts in Peru, and headed west, relying only on the prevailing winds. The dramatic account of his adventure is impossible to put down and is a testament to the power of one man's vision.

Hockenberry, John
⇨ *Moving Violations: War Zones, Wheelchairs, and Declarations of Independence.* 1995. Hyperion, ISBN 0786860782, 371p. AW.

Millions have heard Hockenberry's radio reportage from around the world without knowing that he is a paraplegic, confined to a wheelchair due to a car accident in his late teens. Fiercely independent, he tells how he set about reconstructing a full and accomplished life without the use of his legs. His candor, wit, and anger make this an inspirational, unforgettable story.

Maathai, Wangari
Unbowed: A Memoir. 2006. Anchor Books, ISBN 9780307263483, 314p.

Nobel Peace Prize laureate Maathai's deep connection to her Kenyan homeland was the foundation for a most remarkable career. In a place and time when girls were rarely educated, she pushed for an education and left Kenya to earn a Ph.D. She became an academic and activist and started the Green Belt movement that spread across Africa as a force for women's rights and democracy. Maathai's straightforward, compassionate memoir is a tribute to individual determination.

Opdyke, Irene Gut, with Jennifer Armstrong
In My Hands: Memories of a Holocaust Rescuer. 1999. Alfred A. Knopf, ISBN 0679891811, 276p. ▢.

Opdyke, teenaged daughter of Polish Catholic parents, was caught up in the brutality of World War II and separated from her family. To survive, she worked for the Red Army and the Germans in virtual slave labor. Despite her own dangerous situation, she helped a group of Jews escape, smuggling them out of a nearby ghetto and hiding them in the home of a German officer. This is a stirring tale of bravery and moral courage.

X, Malcolm, with the assistance of Alex Haley
The Autobiography of Malcolm X. 1992 (1965). Ballantine Books, ISBN 0345379756, 500p. 📖.

    Malcolm X grew up in Boston in the 1930s, was expelled from school at 13 and became a drug addict, thief, and pimp. Imprisoned at 21, he began to study and correspond with Elijah Muhammad, leader of the Nation of Islam. Once out of jail, he became a charismatic national figure, speaking out for black empowerment and against integration. An extremely controversial figure, his radical views were inspiring to his supporters, anathema to others. Haley put this autobiography together from taped interviews shortly before Malcolm's assassination in 1965.

Mothers and Daughters, Mothers and Sons

Mothers are powerful people in our lives and in our memoirs too. Several of these authors have found that looking back at their mothers' lives helped them understand themselves. Others pay tribute to remarkable women.

Bragg, Rick
⇨ *All Over But the Shoutin'.* 1997. Pantheon, ISBN 0679442588, 329p. AW.

    Brought up in Georgia near the Alabama border, in beautiful Appalachian Mountain country, Bragg tells the story of his mother's struggle to raise her three boys. Bragg's father was mostly absent, a frightening rage-filled presence when he turned up. In writing this tribute to his mother, Bragg tells his own tale and paints a picture of a bygone Southern era. His writes about his volatile father in another memoir, *The Prince of Frogtown.*

Ellroy, James
My Dark Places: An L.A. Crime Memoir. 1996. Alfred A. Knopf, ISBN 0679441859 351p.

    Ellroy's account of his mother's sordid death and the effect it had on his life reads like a noirish crime novel, cool on the surface and filled with crime sheet facts. The murder left the young Ellroy with an obsessive interest in murdered women and brought him back to the scene of the crime years later to try to learn the truth. Ellroy is also the author of gritty crime fiction.

Gordon, Mary

Circling My Mother. 2007. Pantheon, ISBN 9780375424564, 254p. 📖.

   In writing about her mother, acclaimed novelist Mary Gordon brings us into a claustrophobic world of Catholic spirituality that influenced and permeated her childhood. Anna Gagliano Gordon was crippled by polio but lived a rich, active life as a smartly dressed working woman, good daughter and sister, and ultimately family breadwinner. Gordon has a remarkable ability to capture the texture of her mother's life and milieu and understand its effect on her own life. Gordon wrote a memoir about her enigmatic father called *The Shadow Man: A Daughter's Search for Her Father.*

Gornick, Vivian

Fierce Attachments: A Memoir. 2005 (1987). Farrar, Straus, and Giroux, ISBN 9780374529963, 203p. AW. 📖.

   The author's close but often difficult relationship with her mother underlies this intense memoir of growing up in a socialist apartment complex in the Bronx in the 1940s and 1950s. Gornick's mother and neighbors offered some unusual life lessons in love, sex, and politics that served as a counterpoint to Gornick's efforts to establish her own identity. Long a classic in the feminist community, it is still a fresh coming-of-age story. Gornick, an acclaimed literary critic, also wrote a memoir of time she spent in Egypt called *In Search of Ali Mahmoud.*

Lyden, Jackie

Daughter of the Queen of Sheba. 1997. Houghton Mifflin, ISBN 0395765315, 257p. 📖.

   Lyden's mother was dazzling in her madness: she could be an over-the-top party girl, Queen of Sheba, or poised to run off with an imaginary boyfriend. But life in the Lyden household had a grim side too, as Lyden and her sisters learned from their brutal stepfather. This is a description of madness and its effects on others told in the lush, sizzling prose of someone who has been burned by close contact.

McBride, James

The Color of Water: A Black Man's Tribute to His White Mother. 2006 (1996). Riverhead Books, ISBN 159448192X, 228p. AW. 📖.

   McBride's white mother had 12 children with 2 black husbands. This indomitable woman was ostracized by her Orthodox Jewish family and often scorned by the African American community, but persevered in her dedication to raising and educating her children despite poverty and discrimination. A unique memoir, it has long been a favorite of book clubs.

Ryan, Terry
The Prize Winner of Defiance, Ohio: How My Mother Raised 10 Kids on 25 Words or Less. 2001. Simon & Schuster, ISBN 0743211227, 351p.

With 10 children and an alcoholic, irresponsible husband, Ryan's mother Evelyn entered—and often won—the jingle and slogan contests held by Dial soap, Paper Mate pens, Kleenex tissues and other companies in the 1950s and 1960s to keep her family afloat. Ryan pays tribute to the wonderful optimism, pluck, and good humor which made her the center of gravity for her children.

Passage to Adulthood:
Coming-of-Age Memoirs

The struggle for self-understanding that takes place in young adulthood has long been the stuff of great novels. It makes great memoirs too! As novelist Graham Greene described it: "There is always one moment in childhood when the door opens and lets the future in."[1] These memoirs provide insight into that transformative period in the writers' early years.

Conroy, Frank
Stop-Time: A Memoir. 1977 (1967). Penguin Books, ISBN 9780140044461, 304p. AW.

Conroy grew up in the 1940s and 1950s shuttling between New York and Florida, in a household that was aimless and half mad. His insightful, literate coming-of-age memoir probes the difficult emotions and relationships of his fractured boyhood with style and insight. Conroy is an acclaimed author, critic, and musician; this memoir, originally published in 1967, has long been considered a classic of the genre.

Conroy, Pat
My Losing Season. 2002. Nan A. Talese, ISBN 0385489129, 402p. 📖.

Popular novelist Conroy tells about his senior year playing basketball at The Citadel and how the game helped him find his way out of a childhood of abuse and violence. Basketball gave him a way to express himself, to go beyond fear and shyness to a place of joy. He profiles the season and his teammates with his trademark storytelling ability in this sometimes searing memoir of humiliation and courage. Readers may also enjoy his novels *The Prince of Tides, The Great Santini,* and *The Water Is Wide,* which all draw on Conroy's memories of his Southern childhood.

Eire, Carlos

Waiting for Snow in Havana: Confessions of a Cuban Boy. 2003. Free Press, ISBN 0743219651, 383p. AW.

In this stylishly written, candid memoir, Eire describes a world that is no more: Havana in the 1950s. The son of a wealthy judge who believed he had been Louis XVI in a former life, Eire attended private schools and fancy birthday parties, but also heard the guns of Fidel's rebels. After Batista's ouster, his parents sent him alone to the United States; the terrible loss of home and family overshadows his bittersweet tale.

Kashner, Sam

When I Was Cool: My Life at the Jack Kerouac School: A Memoir. 2004. HarperCollins, ISBN 0060005661, 318p.

Teenage Sam Kashner, writing poetry on Long Island in the 1970s, discovered the Beat poets and followed his heart to Boulder, Colorado, to be a student at the Jack Kerouac School of Disembodied Poetics. In this affectionate, warts-and-all memoir, the shy Kashner recounts how he learned about himself, sex, and celebrity, from Allen Ginsburg, William Burroughs, Gregory Corso, and other aging Beats.

McCarthy, Mary

Memories of a Catholic Girlhood. 1957. Harcourt, Brace, Jovanovich, ISBN 0156586509, 245p. AW. 📖.

McCarthy's painful, beautiful memoir follows her childhood from the loss, at six years old, of both parents in the 1918 influenza epidemic to five years spent with a brutal aunt and uncle, then to her grandparents' house in Seattle. At the Seattle Catholic schools she attended, she struggled with issues of faith and began to develop the insight into women's lives and the intellectual depth that characterized her novels.

Simon, Kate

Bronx Primitive: Portraits in a Childhood. 1982. Viking Press, ISBN 0670192392, 179p.

Simon's perceptive eye for nuance and detail illuminates this classic autobiography of growing up in an immigrant neighborhood in the Bronx in the 1930s, separating from parents, and striking out on one's own path. This is the first in a trilogy that follows her into early adulthood. The other titles are *A Wider World: Portraits in an Adolescence* and *Etchings in an Hourglass.*

Umrigar, Thrity
First Darling of the Morning: Selected Memories of an Indian Childhood.
2004. HarperCollins, ISBN 8172234635, 294p. 📖.

Novelist Umrigar grew up in a middle-class Parsi family in Bombay, surrounded by her father's extended family, well-loved but caught in the undercurrents of family quarrels and jealousies. Umrigar tells how she navigated these difficult waters, but the joy of the memoir is in her exceptionable ability to show us her intellectual development—how she became politically aware and discovered the wonders of literature, art, and music. Umrigar's sensitive, poignant portrait of coming-of-age in Bombay will resonate for readers everywhere.

Wolff, Tobias
⇨ *This Boy's Life.* 1989. Atlantic Monthly Press, ISBN 0871132486, 288p. AW.

Wolff opens this intense, beautifully crafted memoir as he and his mother are traveling west to escape from her violent boyfriend. In Washington State, Wolff spent his teenage years locked in a battle of wills with an abusive stepfather, desperately creating a self that could escape and survive intact. Wolff's insight into his teenage years and the bizarre behavior of the adults around him makes this a tour de force of the genre, by turns chilling and funny. Readers interested in what happened next may get a glimpse in Wolff's autobiographical novel, *Old School,* about a boy at Harvard. His memoir *In Pharaoh's Army: Memories of the Lost War* covers his experiences in Vietnam.

Wright, Richard
Black Boy: A Record of Childhood and Youth. 2006 (1945). HarperPerennial Modern Classics, ISBN 978006113024, 228p. 📖.

Far-reaching in its influence on succeeding generations of African American writers, this is no dry classic, but a powerful, engrossing, and polished narrative of growing up in the early 20th century segregated South. In the originally published ending, Wright heads north; the restored version adds the text of his life in Chicago and completes the bleak vision of the effects of racism.

Then There Were Two: Love and Marriage

How and why we fall in love and marry is one of life's great mysteries, endlessly fascinating in fiction and nonfiction. These memoirs of romantic love run the gamut from idyllic to sad to frightful—there's something for everyone.

Bayley, John
Elegy For Iris. 1999. St. Martin's Press, ISBN 0312198647, 275p. 📖.

Murdoch was an Oxford don, author of more than 20 brilliant philosophical novels on the nature of love and human connection. A free spirit, she and literary critic John Bayley had an unconventional but loving marriage for 40 years. When Murdoch began suffering from memory loss due to Alzheimer's disease, Bayley was determined to maintain their life as best he could, caring for her with great tenderness and searching for traces of who she once was. Truthful and compassionate, Bayley's insight and patience are inspirational.

Hastings, Michael
I Lost My Love in Baghdad: A Modern War Story. 2008. Scribner, ISBN 9781416560975, 276p.

Shortly before journalist Hastings went to Baghdad for *Newsweek,* he met Andi, and sparks flew. In Iraq, Hastings missed Andi but relished his job interviewing Iraqis, traveling with American soldiers, and doing his best to stay alive. When Andi followed him to Baghdad as an aid worker, the violence that he had been reporting came too close to home.

Irwin, Terri
Steve & Me. 2007. Simon Spotlight Entertainment, ISBN 9781416953883, 273p.

The real life story of "The Crocodile Hunter," the remarkable Steve Irwin,, told by his wife Terri, is filled with the stuff of legends. Steve began handling crocodiles at the age of nine and devoted his life to wildlife conservation. Their crocodile-trapping honeymoon became the first episode of a television series; their happy life together was filled with animal rescue work until his untimely death.

Radziwill, Carole
What Remains: A Memoir of Fate, Friendship, and Love. 2005. Scribner, ISBN 9780743276948, 264p.

Radziwill invokes the goddess Fortune and asks the reader to judge if she and her husband, "the small-town working girl and the Polish prince," have been favored. Good times with friends and family and a happy marriage quickly give way to tragedy in this haunting and vivid story. Radziwill's entrée into the world of European and American aristocracy is a fairy tale with a tragic ending.

Sanderson, Catherine

Petite Anglaise: A True Story. 2008. Spiegel & Grau, ISBN 9780385522809, 292p.

Sanderson fulfilled a childhood dream when she moved to Paris; a job, a French boyfriend (Mr. Frog), and then a baby (Tadpole) completed the picture. When the relationship soured and the realities of juggling job and motherhood paled too, she poured her heart out on her blog, Petite Anglaise. Immersion in the blogosphere brought her a lover and life changes. Questions about privacy and voyeurism hover over this frothy, postmodern tale.

Sheffield, Rob

Love Is a Mix Tape: Life and Loss, One Song at a Time. 2007. Crown Publishers, ISBN 9781400083022, 224p.

When shy, nerdy Rob Sheffield met Renée in graduate school, he knew that someone wonderful had entered his life. She was a southern girl with a "noisy, juicy, sparkly life;" their shared passion for the music of the 1990s brought these two different souls together. Sheffield heads each chapter with a list of titles from their mix tapes, riffing off the songs to tell the funny, warm stories of their relationship until its incomprehensible end. Sheffield's tribute to Renée and the music they shared perfectly captures the role that music plays in our lives.

Spencer, Irene

Shattered Dreams: My Life as a Polygamist's Wife. 2007. Center Street, ISBN 9781599957197, 385p.

Spencer grew up believing in the Celestial Law that promised Mormon men glory in God's kingdom if they practiced polygamy. Her mother, one of four wives, encouraged Spencer to avoid a polygamous union, but at 15 she married a man who ultimately had 10 wives. They lived in primitive conditions in Mexico, where she bore 14 children and endured soul-destroying physical and emotional strains before she was able to reclaim her life. This is an unsettling memoir of the dark side of religious faith.

Winik, Marion

⇨ *First Comes Love.* 1996. Pantheon, ISBN 0679445722, 258p. 📖.

In this searing memoir of love doomed by drugs and AIDS, Winik takes us deep into her relationship with Tony, her openly gay husband and soulmate. They met during Mardi Gras, married and had two sons, their relationship swinging wildly between happiness and betrayal. Winik's candid and affecting account of her years with Tony is filled with laughter and pain, told by an unusually insightful writer. Readers who enjoy Winik's confessional writing style may also like her first memoir, *Telling,* or her collection of personal essays, *The Lunch-Box Chronicles: Notes from the Parenting Underground.*

Who Goes There? Struggling with Mental Illness

What is the connection between mind and body? How do mental illness, aging, accidents, and disease affect our brain and change our personalities? Share the thoughts of these authors as they wrestle with these questions from their own experiences.

Armstrong, Karen

The Spiral Staircase: My Climb Out of Darkness. 2004. Alfred A. Knopf, ISBN 0375413189, 305p.

Fans of Armstrong's insightful books about world religions and spirituality may be surprised by this poignant account of her struggles with faith and illness. At 17 she entered a convent, but seven years later she left in despair, lost and depressed, suffering unexplained fainting and amnesiac spells. Not until her illness was diagnosed was she able to create the life that has sustained her and brought her success.

Dorris, Michael

The Broken Cord. 1989. Harper & Row, ISBN 0060160713, 300p. **AW**.

In 1971, Dorris adopted Adam, a Native American three-year-old who was small for his age and developmentally delayed. Dorris believed that love and patience would cure Adam's problems, but no amount of compassion could overcome the disabling effects of fetal alcohol syndrome. Dorris's heartrending memoir of his years with Adam is also filled with anger over the abuse of alcohol in the Native American community.

Grandin, Temple

Thinking in Pictures, Expanded Edition: My Life with Autism. 2006. Vintage Books, ISBN 9780307275653, 270p. 📖.

It is not often that memoirs provide insight into the nature of human understanding and emotion, but Grandin's does just that, as she describes the way she converts all language into visual images that she can recall, replay, and manipulate at will. Despite huge deficits in understanding human interaction, she found mentors who recognized her special talents and she became one of the foremost designers of humane livestock handling equipment. With Grandin's help, we understand that there are many ways to comprehend the world.

Greenberg, Michael
Hurry Down Sunshine. 2008. Other Press, ISBN 9781590511916, 234p.

One summer night Greenberg's 15-year-old daughter Sally had a psychotic breakdown and became a stranger to her frightened father. Care at a psychiatric ward, drug regimens, and talk therapy ultimately provided some relief and stability, but Sally's life was forever changed. With eloquence and compassion, Greenberg recounts his attempts to hold his family together and understand Sally's disease.

Jamison, Kay Redfield
⇨ *An Unquiet Mind: A Memoir of Moods and Madness.* 1995. Alfred A. Knopf, ISBN 0679443746, 223p. 📖.

Jamison had a volatile temperament as a child, but it was not until her teens that she began the wild mood swings of serious manic-depressive illness. Despite the frenzied highs and debilitating lows, she obtained a Ph.D. in psychology and began a successful academic and clinical career studying mood disorders. It took a suicide attempt and a gifted psychiatrist for her to accept medication and come to terms with the benefits and losses of her illness. Jamison gives a very personal, poignant, and absorbing account of what the disease has meant in her life.

Kaysen, Susana
Girl, Interrupted. 1993. Turtle Bay Books, ISBN 0679423664, 168p. **AW**.

At the age of 18, Kaysen was diagnosed with borderline personality disorder and sent to McLean Hospital, where she spent the next two years on a ward for teenage girls. Her descriptions of her time there take the reader into a strange shifting world where the line between sanity and insanity, illness and recovery, is never quite clear.

Skloot, Floyd
In the Shadow of Memory. 2003. Univ. of Nebraska Press, ISBN 0803242972, 243p. 📖.

"I am sometimes a stranger to myself," says Skloot, who was an athlete, poet, novelist, and financial manager when a virus struck his brain and derailed his life in his early 40s. Challenged by the simplest mental and physical tasks, he was compelled to reexamine who he had become and remake his life. With moving honesty and eloquence, he provides this exquisite meditation on the relationship between brain and mind, the role of memory in making us who we are, and how our childhoods shape our adult lives.

Williams, Donna

Nobody Nowhere: The Extraordinary Autobiography of an Autistic. 1992. Times Books, ISBN 0812920422, 219p.

Williams's struggle to understand and function in the world around her is all the more meaningful to us because unlike many autistics she is able to express her inner life so clearly. She grew up in Australia, the daughter of abusive parents, locked in a world of fantasy and hallucination. When she was in her mid-20s, she found a therapist who helped her understand and relate to the world around her. A heartbreaking and exhilarating story of what it means to live with a disability. A second memoir, *Somebody, Somewhere: Breaking Free from the World of Autism,* follows her into adulthood and teaching career.

Note

1. Graham Greene. *The Power and the Glory.* 1940. Reprinted with preface by John Updike. New York: Penguin Classics, 2003, p. 12.

Chapter Two

Story

Without the element of risk—*risk that something will go wrong*—there is no story.
Unlearning to Fly, Jennifer Brice

"It's amazing how you remember everything so clearly," a woman said... "All those conversations, details. Were you ever worried that you might get something wrong?"

"I didn't remember it," Lucy said presently. "I wrote it. I'm a writer."
Ann Patchett, *Truth and Beauty*

Readers who are looking for a good story will find it in these memoirs, full of events that sweep us along. We're eager to learn how the author survived, coped, and changed. We're in the writer's hands, along for a great narrative ride.

These memoirs have a strong narrative line with a beginning where the author sets the scene and draws us in, a middle that develops the story, and an end that—usually—provides closure. We may only learn as much about the author's life as is relevant to the story; that's all we need to know. Events and action are emphasized over character development and many of the authors use dialogue to advance the storyline.

Every genre of fiction is represented in this chapter. Andrea Giovino's *Divorced from the Mob* reads like a thriller; Rinker Buck's *Flight of Passage* is a great adventure story; Rachel Simon's *Riding the Bus with My Sister* is a heartwarming family story; and Vera Brittain's *Testament of Youth* will satisfy readers who enjoy historical fiction. These life stories may be fast-paced or leisurely; humorous or dark, literary or colloquial. What they have in common is an emphasis on a tale to be told.

Crooked Lives: People Behaving Badly

These are memoirs of people behaving badly, in business or personal life. Are we shocked? Maybe, but not enough to stop reading their compulsively interesting stories.

Alson, Peter
Confessions of an Ivy League Bookie: True Tales of Love and the Vig. 1996. Crown Publishers, ISBN 0517703300, 228p.

At 33, Alson was at a dead end. The Harvard graduate had left his girlfriend Anna in Chicago and returned to New York, but couldn't find work; then he ran into Michael, who was earning six figures as a bookie. Alson started taking bets in Michael's office, getting deeper into the seedy business until the day the police broke up the party. Fast-paced, filled with characters with names like "Monkey" and "Tuna," Alson tells a breezy story of easy money and bad choices.

Cohen, Rich
⇨ *Sweet and Low: A Family Story.* 2006. Farrar, Straus and Giroux, ISBN 9780374272296, 272p.

When calorie counting became the rage, Ben Eisenstadt's sugar substitute was in the sweet spot. Millions of those familiar pink packets poured off the assembly line of the Brooklyn factory daily. This classic story of the ups and downs of a three-generation family-owned business has a unique cast of cantankerous and shady characters. Cohen, from the disinherited side of the family, tells a funny, bittersweet tale.

Fenton, Peter
Eyeing the Flash: The Education of a Carnival Con Artist. 2005. Simon & Schuster, ISBN 0743258541, 244p.

Fenton was a nerdy teen, good at math but socially inept, and with inattentive, alcoholic parents. He was ripe for friendship with the sly Jackie Barron, whose grifter parents ran a traveling carnival. Barron taught Fenton the art of the con and he took to it with gusto, dropping down into the seamy carny life.

This is a fast-paced story with colorful characters, snappy dialogue, and an inside look at a tawdry world.

Geng, Steve

Thick as Thieves: A Brother, a Sister—A True Story of Two Turbulent Lives. 2007. Henry Holt, ISBN 9780805080568, 292p. 📖.

Growing up as army brats, Geng and his sister, the writer Veronica Geng, were close, but by adulthood their lives couldn't have been more different: he was a down-and-out drug addict and petty thief and she was a part of the literary scene at *The New Yorker,* successful but emotionally fragile. Geng tells a brash, unapologetic tale of his wild life with the bravado of a survivor.

Giovino, Andrea, with Gary Brozek

Divorced from the Mob: My Journey from Organized Crime to Independent Woman. 2004. Carroll & Graf, ISBN 9780786713554, 258p.

Giovino grew up in a Brooklyn neighborhood where power and respect came from mob connections. Her mother sent her out to steal milk and bread for her nine brothers and sisters and encouraged her to find a man like the well-dressed mobsters who gambled in their basement. Her liaisons and marriages with well-connected drug dealers and killers brought her a life right out of *The Sopranos* until the DEA knocked on the door. Giovino pulls no punches and makes no apologies in this compelling, page-turning tale.

Hansen, Suzanne

You'll Never Nanny in This Town Again: The True Adventures of a Hollywood Nanny. 2005. Crown Publishers, ISBN 0307237540, 289p.

A small-town Oregon girl, Hansen headed for Los Angeles to find her dream job as a live-in nanny to the stars. Her first job with mega-agent Michael Ovitz's family was an eye-opener: these Hollywood celebs couldn't be bothered spending time with their children, they nickel-and-dimed her, kept her on call 24/7, and threatened her when she gave notice. Happier times ensued, but the humor and charm in this exposé keep on coming.

Israel, Lee

Can You Ever Forgive Me? Memoirs of a Literary Forger. 2008. Simon & Schuster, ISBN 9781416588672, 129p.

Short and sharp, Israel's unapologetic memoir of how she forged letters of literary celebrities to support herself makes a delicious read. Noel Coward, Dorothy Parker, and Lillian Hellman were among those whose correspondence was enriched by Israel's well-researched, spicy contributions. Some of the 300 letters she forged are probably yet to be revealed as fakes.

Kingsland, Rosemary

The Secret Life of a Schoolgirl. 2003. Crown Publishers, ISBN 140004782X, 343p.

Kingsland's story is like a rich meal, stuffed with passion, outrageous characters, and unsettling events. She left India as a young girl in 1948, and lived in various parts of England while her parents' marriage crashed on the rocks of adultery and alcoholism. The tantalizing secret she kept for 40 years, revealed in engrossing detail here, is her affair at the age of 13 with the actor Richard Burton.

Stapinski, Helene

Five Finger Discount: A Crooked Family History. 2001. Random House, ISBN 0679463062, 260p.

Hudson County, New Jersey, was infamous for crime and corruption and Jersey City was the jewel in its crown. Stapinski, who grew up there in the 1970s, recounts with humor and irony how her family benefited from patronage schemes but also suffered at the hands of corrupt police and politicians. Her father brought home lobster tails and steaks that "fell off the truck" and Grandpa Beansie, a convicted murderer, filched encyclopedias from the free public library. This is a raucous tale of a childhood spent among lawless, eccentric, and heartbreaking characters.

Young, Toby

How to Lose Friends and Alienate People. 2002. Da Capo Press, ISBN 030681188X, 340p.

Young moved from London to New York to enter the high stakes world of celebrity journalism, but in his misguided efforts, lost his dream job at *Vanity Fair* and offended anyone of use to his career. His breezy, no-holds-barred portraits of his own failings and the backstabbing, driven people he met is highly entertaining. Lots of name dropping for fans of *The Devil Wears Prada;* the book was also made into a movie.

Dishing: Stories from the Kitchen

In this era of celebrity chefs and celebrity restaurateurs, we're more curious than ever about the food business. At the same time, we're watching what we eat more carefully. So, here's the question: can reading about eating substitute for the real thing? Taste these memoirs from well-known chefs and foodies.

Bourdain, Anthony

Kitchen Confidential: Adventures in the Culinary Underbelly. 2000. Bloomsbury, ISBN 158234082X, 307p.

The bad boy of New York chefs tells all in this hectic memoir of his culinary adventures, good, bad, and ugly, including advice on what not to eat in restaurants and why. You'll laugh at the pranks, you'll gasp at the bad taste of this in-your-face page turner whose pace never flags. The names of restaurants and chefs are disguised, but real foodies will recognize the cast.

Buford, Bill

⇨ *Heat: An Amateur's Adventures as Kitchen Slave, Line Cook, Pasta-Maker, and Apprentice to a Dante-Quoting Butcher in Tuscany.* 2006. Alfred A. Knopf, ISBN 9781400041206, 318p.

In his forties, Buford left the literary life to immerse himself in Italian cooking, joining the crew at Mario Batali's Babbo restaurant in New York as a kitchen slave. He became obsessed with understanding the origins of traditional Italian cookery and sought apprenticeships with an Italian pasta maker and butcher. His fast-paced, ebullient, self-deprecating, spirited tale is filled with larger-than-life eccentric and driven characters, details about the history and techniques of Italian cookery, and the quest for the perfect meal. Buford loves to immerse himself in a subject; in an earlier book, *Among the Thugs,* he traveled around Europe with British soccer hooligans.

Child, Julia, with Alex Prud'homme

My Life in France. 2006. Alfred A. Knopf, ISBN 9781400043460, 317p.

We're so lucky that Julia Child kept a journal of her first years in France! With the assistance of her grand-nephew, Alex, we have this delightful record of newly married Julia eating her first French meal, falling in love with Paris, enrolling in cooking school, and finding her vocation. The frank tone recalls Julia's distinctive voice and flair, and provides insight into the roots of the later, very public Julia.

Damrosch, Phoebe

Service Included: Four-Star Secrets of an Eavesdropping Waiter. 2007. Wm. Morrow, ISBN 9780061228148, 256p.

Foodie Damrosch gets the job of a lifetime at Per Se restaurant, star chef Thomas Keller's entrée into the stratospheric reaches of New York dining.

During intensive training to be the perfect backserver, she falls for sommelier André. The pressure cooker world of fine dining—how many stars will *The New York Times* reviewer dole out?—is crossed with an exuberant chick lit story of love and longing in Manhattan.

Hazan, Marcella
Amarcord—Marcella Remembers: The Story of a Woman Who Started Out to Teach Science in a Small Town in Italy, but Ended Up Teaching America How to Cook Italian. 2008. Gotham Books, ISBN 9781592403882, 307p.

Hazan, doyenne of Italian cooking in America and author of *The Classic Italian Cookbook,* reflects on her long and varied life, beginning with her childhood in Alexandria, Egypt, and Cesenatico, Italy. She was aiming for a medical career until she met husband Victor, who brought her to the United States. In 1969, looking for something to do, she offered cooking classes in her home; *The New York Times* food critic Craig Claiborne arrived one day and her career was launched. Hazan's warm and winning memoir is full of the joy of food, family, and friends.

Pepin, Jacques
The Apprentice: My Life in the Kitchen. 2003. Houghton Mifflin, ISBN 0618197370, 318p.

Pepin's ebullient story starts in a French village where he worked in his mother's restaurants. He began a series of apprenticeships at age 13 and in his early twenties was chef to Charles de Gaulle. Looking to expand his horizons, he came to New York, where he fell in with the right crowd: Craig Claiborne, Pierre Franey, Julia Child, and others who were revolutionizing American home cooking. Franey's self-described charmed life stems from a buoyant personality, luck, and great talent.

Reichl, Ruth
Tender at the Bone: Growing Up at the Table. 1998. Random House, ISBN 0679449876, 282p. 📖.

Reichl, now editor of *Gourmet Magazine,* recounts how her childhood experiences put food front and center in her life. Her mother was a famously awful cook who emptied the contents of the refrigerator into one pot to make dinner. Cooking, for Reichl, was a matter of survival. In Berkeley during the food revolution of the 1970s she blossomed into a food critic. Reichl tells delicious stories of people and meals and includes recipes. She followed this memoir with two more: *Comfort Me with Apples: More Adventures at the Table* and *Garlic and Sapphires: The Secret Life of a Critic in Disguise.*

Slater, Nigel

Toast: The Story of a Boy's Hunger. 2004. Gotham Books, ISBN 1592400906, 238p.

British cookbook author Slater writes with delicious intimacy about the food of his childhood, especially the sweets: candies, crumbles, trifles, and puddings. Through heartbreaking and funny vignettes of meals and holidays we come to know his awkward, asthmatic mother and difficult father. Slater candidly admits that "food is the blood in my memoir's veins;" it is also how he reveals the sad details of his mother's early death and his own struggles to break free of his family.

Faultlines: Difficult Family Relationships

These are the memoirs we love to read and weep over, written by survivors of unhappy family experiences. They're filled with drama and angst, but also with the insight of the survivor.

Carroll, James

An American Requiem: God, My Father, and the War that Came Between Us. 1996. Houghton Mifflin, ISBN 039577926X, 279p. AW. 📖.

The Vietnam War pitted son against father in many families and Carroll's stance as an anti-war priest was particularly painful for his father, an Air Force general. In this penetrating, introspective memoir, Carroll describes his childhood love of all things military, the complex family dynamics that led him to the priesthood, and the pain of estrangement from his father. He reminds us of the personal cost of dissent in that turbulent era when religion was often on the front lines of political protest.

Gilmore, Mikal

Shot in the Heart. 1994. Doubleday, ISBN 0385422938, 403p. AW. 📖.

Violence begets violence in this lurid story about convicted murderer Gary Gilmore and his family, penned by his younger brother in an effort to understand without excusing. Gilmore's mother was the victim of violence as a child, his father was also abused and the perpetrator of violence as a husband and father. Gilmore's story of his supremely dysfunctional family is hypnotically fascinating.

Karr, Mary

The Liar's Club: A Memoir. 1995. Viking Press, ISBN 0670850535, 320p.
AW. 📖.

Karr's bleak tale of family dysfunction struck a chord with readers and writers when it was published, opening the door to a flood of family memoirs. She grew up in a swampy west Texas oil town with mismatched alcoholic parents: a mother who practiced serial marriage and a father who presided over the aptly named Liar's Club. The intensity of Karr's prose along with her scrappy, tough-mindedness combine to make a riveting story. The memoir of her teenage years is titled *Cherry.*

MacDonald, Michael Patrick

⇨ *All Souls: A Family Story from Southie.* 1999. Beacon Press, ISBN 0807072125, 266p. 📖.

For some, this story of life in the Old Colony projects in South Boston would be a tragic tale, but for MacDonald, Southie was a place where he felt part of a protective Irish community. Never mind that he and his eight siblings had three different—all absent—fathers, that ambulances into Old Colony required a police escort, or that drug-related violence claimed the lives of many dear to him. This memoir of growing up in a raw and explosive community is a riveting family tale and an indictment of our society's inability to deal with poverty.

Mori, Kyoko

The Dream of Water: A Memoir. 1995. Henry Holt, ISBN 0805032606, 275p. 📖.

Mori returned to Japan after a long absence, full of conflicting emotions. Her mother committed suicide when she was a child and her father was distant and abusive, her stepmother manipulative. In returning to places where she lived and talking to relatives about that unhappy time, she tries to forgive and forget. This is an unsettling, honest account of the sadness of bridging two cultures and the effects of destructive family relationships.

Sheehan, Andrew

Chasing the Hawk: Looking for My Father, Finding Myself. 2001. Delacorte Press, ISBN 038533561X, 291p.

Dr. George Sheehan was an inspiration to runners; he came to the sport at midlife with intense passion and a gift for writing about its joys and benefits that brought him fame and media adulation. His son's memoir reveals the darker side of the legend: Sheehan was an intense, absent father whose selfish pursuit of his own needs left his son with no anchor. The son was an alcoholic by his twenties, his life was in tatters until his father, dying of cancer, miraculously reached out to help.

Four Seasons: Memoirs of One Year

The memoirs in this list have one thing in common: they cover one year in the life of the author. There's something about coming full circle, back to the season where we started that encourages reflection and provides a satisfying sense of accomplishment.

Adams, Noah
> *Piano Lessons: Music, Love & True Adventures.* 1996. Delacorte Press, ISBN 0385314043, 250p.
>
>> Popular NPR host Adams describes his year of learning to play the piano, fulfilling a lifelong dream of creating music. Along with descriptions of his struggles at the keyboard, we learn about famous pianists and the history of the piano. When he surprises his wife at the end of the year by playing Schumann's *Traumerei,* we share his exultation.

Becker, Suzy
> *I Had Brain Surgery, What's Your Excuse?: An Illustrated Memoir.* 2004. Workman Publishing, ISBN 0761124780, 282p.
>
>> Becker, cartoonist and author of *All I Need to Know I Learned from My Cat,* writes about her brain surgery and the year of recovery that followed with warmth and insight. Delightfully quirky illustrations chart her progress and reveal her inner demons. Doctors assured her before surgery that she would have no aftereffects but she suffered from frightening speech and language problems. Her efforts to deal with the issue of who we are when we lose certain of our attributes will resonate with all readers.

Duane, Daniel
> *Caught Inside: A Surfer's Year on the California Coast.* 1996. North Point Press, ISBN 086547494X, 239p.
>
>> Duane's at loose ends, a 20-something working at a sports shop in Berkeley, when he packs it all in for a year of surfing around Monterey Bay. He starts with a hand-me-down board and wetsuit, honing his rusty skills and learning

how to read the weather and waves. The glorious California coast is the backdrop to a quiet but absorbing year of personal discovery, served up with lots of surfing lore, lyrically told.

Mayle, Peter, illustrated by Judith Clancy

A Year in Provence. 1990. Alfred A. Knopf, ISBN 0394572300, 207p. 📖.

After years of visiting France as tourists, Mayle and his wife bought a stone farmhouse in the Luberon region, moved in, and began to restore it. Their adventures with craftsmen, neighbors, local characters, and delicious food fill this delightful paean to the French countryside and way of life.

Powell, Julie

Julie and Julia: 365 Days, 524 Recipes, 1 Tiny Apartment Kitchen. 2005. Little, Brown and Co., ISBN 031610969X, 309p. 📖.

Powell challenged herself to cook all 524 recipes in Julia Child's *Mastering the Art of French Cooking* in one year and blog about her experiences. She vowed to find all the ingredients, no matter how obscure, and master every cooking technique. She recounts how her adventure, which she began in the hopes that it would revitalize her marriage and restore her soul, was a richly rewarding experience.

Shah, Tahir

The Caliph's House: A Year in Casablanca. 2006. Bantam Books, ISBN 0553803999, 349p.

Shah fell in love with an abandoned, decaying house in exotic Casablanca, filled with beautiful gardens and courtyards, and uprooted his family from London. He optimistically started repair work, but the house had guardians and enemies—human and spiritual—that needed to be appeased. In a year, Shah and his family learned many cross-cultural lessons from a unique and bizarre cast of characters. Shah's second book on Morocco, *In Arabian Nights: A Caravan of Moroccan Dreams,* melds family stories with Moroccan folklore.

Simon, Rachel

⇨ *Riding the Bus with My Sister: A True Life Journey.* 2002. Houghton Mifflin, ISBN 0618045996, 296p. 📖.

Simon's sister Beth has mental retardation and spends her days riding the buses in the small city where she lives on her own. She invites Simon to join her a few days each month for a year; the experience gives Simon a deeper understanding of Beth's life and opens a window on the family traumas of the past, healing and helping both sisters.

Ward, Logan

See You in a Hundred Years: Four Seasons in Forgotten America. 2006. Ben-
Bella Books, ISBN 1933771151, 245p. 📖.

Ward, a freelance writer, and his wife Heather, grew tired of the New
York rat race and opted out for a year to live on a Virginia farm with their
toddler. Their goal was to transport themselves back to 1900: they traded their
car for a horse and wagon, ripped out plumbing and electricity, and lived off
the land. Skeptical neighbors turned into a community as Ward's hopes for a
renewing year came to fruition.

In Harm's Way: Lives at Risk

These absorbing memoirs tell of people who survived extremely difficult
situations by their wits, luck, and the kindness of strangers. Some were trapped
by political and social upheavals, born in the wrong time and place. Others held
political views that put their lives in danger. One author knowingly placed himself in a life-threatening situation.

Chang, Jung

Wild Swans: Three Daughters of China. 1991. Simon & Schuster, ISBN
0671685465, 524p. 📖.

Chang, her mother, and grandmother lived turbulent lives, caught up in the
violent winds of change buffeting 20th-century China. Her grandmother was a
warlord's concubine with bound feet and her mother fought with the Communist underground as a teenager, devoting her life to the Party despite periods of
ostracism. Chang herself was caught up in the Cultural Revolution and saw her
family reviled. Her memoir is full of drama, a personal and historical record of
remarkable people and times.

Delaney, Bob, with Dave Scheiber

Covert: My Years Infiltrating the Mob. 2008. Sterling, ISBN 9781402754432,
276p.

In the mid-1970s, Delaney was an undercover officer building a case
against the Mob on the New Jersey waterfront, living a double life as Bobby
Covert, president of a trucking company with Mob connections, and wearing a wire. Now an NBA referee, he still bears the emotional scars of his descent into an ugly world of fear and extortion. This real-life thriller is a fast,
riveting read.

Hahn-Beer, Edith, and Susan Dworkin

The Nazi Officer's Wife: How One Jewish Woman Survived the Holocaust. 1999. Rob Weisbach Books/William Morrow, ISBN 068816689X, 305p. 📖.

Hahn-Beer's story is riveting and compulsively readable. After deportation to the Viennese ghetto and several stints in labor camps, she became a "U-boat," passing as a non-Jew in wartime Germany, trying to find work and stay alive. In the most incredible turn of events, marriage to a willing but volatile Nazi officer provided her with precarious protection to ride out the war.

Mathabane, Mark

Kaffir Boy: The True Story of a Black Youth's Coming of Age in Apartheid South Africa. 1998 (1986). Simon & Schuster, ISBN 0684848287, 354p.

In this classic account, Mathabane tells how he grew up in a nightmarish ghetto in Johannesburg under the brutal, repressive apartheid regime, where violence from gangs and police cut short the lives of many young men. Driven by dreams of education and freedom, he became a tennis player and won a scholarship to an American university. His story is continued in *Kaffir Boy in America.*

Rawicz, Slavomir

⇨ *The Long Walk: The True Story of a Trek to Freedom.* 1997 (1956). Lyons Press, ISBN 1558216340, 242p.

Rawicz was in the Polish army in 1939 when he was arrested by the Russians as a spy, tortured, and transferred to a labor camp in Siberia. He organized an escape with six other prisoners and they trekked south, from Siberia to India, across the Gobi Desert and the Himalayas. The story of how they worked together to survive is simply told and impossible to put down.

Salbi, Zainab, with Laurie Becklund

Between Two Worlds: Escape from Tyranny: Growing Up in the Shadow of Saddam. 2005. Gotham Books, ISBN 1592401562, 295p.

Salbi tells a chilling story of growing up in Iraq, focusing on the time when her father was Saddam Hussein's private pilot. Saddam ordered her family to spend weekends in a house on the palace grounds, where they were at his beck and call. Salbi's mother taught her to call him Amo (uncle), forget dangerous information, wear a plastic smile, and live with fear as others around them were murdered at Saddam's whim.

Szpilman, Wladyslaw, trans. by Anthea Bell

The Pianist: The Extraordinary True Story of One Man's Survival in Warsaw,
1939–1945, with Extracts from the Diary of Wilm Hosenfeld. 1999. Picador
USA, ISBN 0312244150, 221p. 📖.

When the Nazis invaded Poland, pianist Szpilman and his family were
forced out of their home into the Warsaw Ghetto. Friends offered Szpilman a
chance to avoid transport to a camp and he spent the war hiding out in empty
apartments, barely surviving, wracked by fear and guilt. He wrote this memoir
just after the war; it is a harrowing tale of desperation and the sustaining power
of music.

Ung, Loung

First They Killed My Father: A Daughter of Cambodia Remembers. 2000.
HarperCollins, ISBN 0060193328, 240p. 📖.

When Ung was five, her family was caught up in the bloody years of
Khmer Rouge control of Cambodia. They were forced to leave their comfortable, middle-class life in Phnom Penh and move around the countryside posing
as peasants and enduring starvation, forced labor, rape, and beatings. They
eventually split up so that some would survive. Ung tells this heartrending
story in the present tense so we share her loneliness, fear, and devastation,
cheering the courageous spirit that carried her through.

Living to Tell the Tale:
Near-Death Experiences

These authors lived through life-threatening experiences, enduring the worst
that man and nature have to offer. They survived to write these vivid stories,
filled with emotion and courage.

Beah, Ishmael

A Long Way Gone: Memoirs of a Boy Soldier. 2007. Farrar, Straus and Giroux,
ISBN 0374105235, 229p. 📖.

Sierra Leone in the 1990s was riven by civil war, a terrifying place to be a
child. Beah was a carefree pre-teen in his small village, memorizing rap songs
from American cassettes, when rebel attacks robbed him of home, friends, and
family. At the age of 12 he was recruited as a child soldier and trained to kill.
His account of this hellish experience and how he survived is beautifully told.

Callahan, Steven

Adrift: 76 Days Lost at Sea. 2002 (1986). Houghton Mifflin, ISBN 0618257322, 237p.

A passionate sailor, Callahan put all his money into building a small sailboat and in 1981 he set off alone across the Atlantic. After six days, his boat sank in a storm and he was left in an inflatable raft with little food and water. Remarkably, he survived a record 76 days fighting off sharks, starvation, and desperation. A classic of seafaring literature.

Cherry-Garrard, Apsley

The Worst Journey in the World: Antarctic 1910–1913. 2005 (1922). Penguin Books, ISBN 0143039385, 573p.

Cherry-Garrard was one of the few survivors of Robert Falcon Scott's ill-fated South Pole expedition in 1910 and one of three to make the famous (and foolhardy) Winter Journey to collect Emperor penguin eggs. His account is measured, even humorous at times, but his vivid stories of how they endured horrific conditions in the service of science is both tragic and inspirational. This classic of adventure literature has been continuously in print since it was published in 1922.

Hall, Lincoln

Dead Lucky: Life After Death on Mount Everest. 2008. Jeremy P. Tarcher/ Penguin, ISBN 9781585426461, 309p.

Hall, an Australian mountain climber, failed to reach the top of Mt. Everest in 1984, but returned for a second chance in 2006. When he collapsed from altitude sickness and appeared dead during the descent, his team went on, but the next morning, in a stunning recovery, sherpas found him very much alive. He tells not only the riveting story of his own climb and hallucinatory near-death experience but provides insight into Mt. Everest's deadly fascination.

Parrado, Nando

⇨ *Miracle in the Andes: 72 Days on the Mountain and My Long Trek Home.* 2006. Crown Publishers, ISBN 9781400097678, 291p. 📖.

In 1972, a team of young Uruguayan rugby players were flying to Chile when their plane crashed in a remote and frigid area of the Andes. Parrado, who survived with a fractured skull, tells how they banded together to outwit the elements for over two months. His very candid account of the ordeal and how he relied for strength on his father's teachings, is gripping and inspirational.

Silverstein, Amy

Sick Girl. 2007. Grove/Atlantic, ISBN 9780802118547, 293p.

At 24, Silverstein was a law school student with a new boyfriend; life was good until she began experiencing blackouts. One terrifying year later, she received a heart transplant and everything about her life was transformed. No simple story of miraculous survival, this memoir takes the reader into the depths of Silverstein's fear and anger and her continuing fight for normalcy.

Simpson, Joe

Touching the Void. 2004 (1988). Perennial, ISBN 0060730552, 218p.

Simpson and his partner Simon Yates were climbing in the Peruvian Andes, heading to the top of a 21,000 foot snow-covered peak to climb down the north ridge, when Simpson fell off an ice ledge, breaking his leg. Yates tried to lower him to safety, but eventually had to cut the rope. How Simpson, frightened, in pain, lashed by a blizzard, crawled to safety is a gripping story of courage and luck

Timerman, Jacobo, trans. by Toby Talbot

Prisoner without a Name, Cell without a Number. 2002 (1981). University of Wisconsin Press, ISBN 0299182444, 164p. `AW`.

In the 1970s, Argentina went through a period of extreme social turmoil and terrorism; thousands of people were murdered and thousands more disappeared. Timerman, arrested by a faction of the army for his advocacy of human rights, was tortured and interrogated for 30 months before being expelled from the country in 1979. Not for the faint of heart, this book describes Timerman's harrowing experience and the climate of repression in Argentina in chilling detail.

Moments of Truth: Stories of Turning Points

Can you recall a moment in your life when everything changed and nothing was ever the same again? In this list, people write about those watershed moments. Some had flashes of insight about themselves or others close to them; others made decisions that would change the course of their lives.

Buck, Rinker

⇨ *Flight of Passage: A True Story.* 1997. Hyperion, ISBN 0786861002, 351p.

Buck's father was a barnstorming pilot who set such high expectations for his sons that in 1966, 15-year-old Buck and his 17-year-old brother refurbished a Piper Cub and flew across country. Their trip was not just an exhilarating stunt, but a rite of passage to free themselves of their father's influence and make peace with their own ambitions. Great storytelling combined with affecting personal history make this a standout.

Carhart, Thaddeus
The Piano Shop on the Left Bank: Discovering a Forgotten Passion. 2001. Random House, ISBN 0375503048, 271p. 📖.

Carhart passed the unobtrusive Paris piano shop daily as he walked his children to school; it reminded him of his love of the piano. Not until he had an introduction from a trusted client was he accepted by Luc, the owner, and admitted to the workroom. Carhart became a regular visitor and bought a piano, delighted to play again. In this charming, informative memoir, we come to know Luc and his devotion to great instruments, Jos, the enigmatic piano tuner, and learn about piano history and construction.

Chapman, Fern Shumer
Motherland: Beyond the Holocaust: A Daughter's Journey to Reclaim the Past. 2000. Viking Press, ISBN 0670881058, 190p. 📖.

In 1938, Chapman's mother was sent alone from Germany to the United States to escape the escalating persecution of Jews. She put the past behind her and never spoke of Germany to her daughter, but the loss was always there, poisoning her life and relationships. When she decided to return to her childhood village, Chapman went with her and together they reclaimed their family history and achieved a measure of catharsis.

Giffels, David
All the Way Home: Building a Family in a Falling-Down House. 2008. Wm. Morrow, ISBN 9780061362866, 314p.

Giffels, looking for a home for his growing family, fell in love with a decaying 1913 mansion in Akron, Ohio, and bought it despite structural problems, animal inhabitants, and non-functional plumbing and electricity. It was a do-it-yourself nightmare, but Giffels and his wife never doubted that the house was meant for them. Funny and tender, this is an exploration of what it means to create a family home.

Hall, Sara
Drawn to the Rhythm: A Passionate Life Reclaimed. 2002. W.W. Norton & Co., ISBN 039304940X, 285p. 📖.

Readers will cheer through their tears as Hall reclaims her life from her psychologically abusive husband in this insightful, absorbing memoir. One day driving along the water with her children, Hall was struck by the grace of a solitary rower and began an early morning training regimen in a borrowed scull, going on to become a champion racer. She gained physical and mental strength, allowing her to "row my way to freedom."

Keneally, Thomas
Searching for Schindler: A Memoir. 2008. Nan A. Talese, ISBN 9780385526173, 272p.

When novelist Keneally stepped into a Beverly Hills handbag and luggage store in 1988, he met Leopold "Poldek" Pfefferberg, a Holocaust survivor with a story he asked Keneally to write. That story became the book and the film *Schindler's List,* about the Nazi officer who risked his own life to save Jews. In this moving memoir, Keneally recounts how he became fascinated with Schindler's story and traveled to Poland, Germany, Austria, and Israel with Pfefferberg to find and interview other Schindler survivors.

McCourt, Frank
Teacher Man: A Memoir. 2005. Scribner, ISBN 9780743243773, 258p.

McCourt's bestselling memoir, *Angela's Ashes,* helped spark a revival of memoir reading and writing with its unsettling glimpse into his early years in Ireland. Readers persevered in spite of the misery it depicted because of his lack of sentimentality. Here, he tells of his days teaching in New York City high schools, struggling to learn the secret of connecting with disaffected teens while finding his own voice as a writer. Told with his trademark wit and irreverence.

Reed, Julia
The House on First Street: My New Orleans Story. 2007. Ecco Press, ISBN 9780061136641, 208p.

Journalist Reed moved to New Orleans in her twenties, an enthusiastic participant in the liquor-soaked decadent lifestyle and a wry connoisseur of its eccentric citizens and nightlife. She and her husband found their dream house in the Garden District, embarked on ambitious renovations, and moved in just a month before Hurricane Katrina. Her breezy tale turns anguished as she recounts efforts to rescue friends and support her beloved city.

Shames, Laurence, and Peter Barton
Not Fade Away: A Short Life Well Lived. 2003. Rodale, ISBN 1579546889, 224p.

Barton lived fast: he protested the Vietnam War in the 1960s, spent time as a ski bum and craps dealer, managed political campaigns, founded a successful media company, and had a loving wife and children. Life was rich until he was diagnosed with stomach cancer in his late forties. With Shames's help and contribution, he reflects on his life and confronts his death with a unique blend of candor, heroism, and humor.

Tucker, Neely
  Love in the Driest Season: A Family Memoir. 2004. Crown Publishers, ISBN 0609609769, 242p.
    In a Zimbabwean orphanage, foreign correspondent Tucker and his wife Vita found Chipo, a critically ill infant girl abandoned at birth. It was love at first sight, but their adoption efforts pitted them against government bureaucrats and cultural taboos. It was only through the fierceness of their love for Chipo that they succeeded. Keep the tissues handy while reading this one.

Off the Beaten Path: Unusual Adventures

If something is difficult, challenging, or even forbidden, someone is sure to rise to the occasion—and write about it. These authors tell how they blazed their own trails, took off on quests, and where it led them.

Grann, David
  The Lost City of Z: A Tale of Deadly Obsession in the Amazon. 2009. Doubleday, ISBN 9780385513531, 339p.
    Like many who were lured deep into the Amazon jungle in search of fabled cities of gold, British explorer Percy Fawcett set off in 1925 to find the city he called Z, but he vanished without a trace. Since then, many have tried to solve the mystery of his disappearance, sometimes with fatal results. Grann set off to try his luck, despite an aversion to the outdoors and a poor sense of direction. He interweaves his own Amazon adventure with the story of Fawcett's expedition.

Harrer, Heinrich, trans. by Richard Graves
  Seven Years in Tibet. 1996 (1954). Penguin Putnam, ISBN 0874778883, 329p. AW.
    Harrer, an Austrian national, mountaineer, and skier, was trapped in the Far East when World War II began, and interned by the British in India. He made a daring escape with a friend, crossed the Himalayas and arrived in Lhasa, then a closed city. Harrer was fascinated with the Tibetan culture and

people, and became the Dalai Lama's tutor, fleeing with him when the Chinese invaded in 1950. In recent years, Harrer's candor has been called into account, but this memoir remains one of the most engaging adventure stories written.

Hillary, Sir Edmund Percival
View From the Summit: The Remarkable Memoir by the First Person to Conquer Everest. 2000. Pocket Books, ISBN 9780743400671, 310p.

In 1953, Hillary became the first person to reach the summit of Mt. Everest, a remarkable feat that captured the imagination of the world and inspired many others to attempt the ascent. Hillary follows up that remarkable story with other adventures—to the South Pole and up the Ganges—in this entertaining story of a life filled with courageous adventures.

Irvine, Lucy
Castaway: A Story of Survival. 1983. Random House, ISBN 0394535421, 288p.

Unconventional Lucy Irvine answered an ad for a "wife" to live for a year as a castaway on the deserted island of Tuin, north of Australia. Although the relationship with George was fraught with tension from the start, Lucy came to love the stark beauty of Tuin and the adventure of surviving off the land. This is a very moving personal tale of physical and emotional survival.

Kane, Joe
⇨ *Running the Amazon.* 1989. Alfred A. Knopf, ISBN 0394553314, 277p.

On a lark, journalist Kane joined the first expedition to attempt to run the entire length of the Amazon River by kayak. The list of challenges was long, including deadly rapids, tropical diseases, and, as it turned out, the personalities of the expedition members. Kane's descriptions of the rigors of the journey match any adventure fiction written.

Krakauer, Jon
Into Thin Air: A Personal Account of the Mount Everest Disaster. 1997. Villard, ISBN 0679457526, 293p. AW. 📖.

Since Mt. Everest was discovered in 1852, climbers have tried to scale it; although many have died in the attempt, there is now a booming business in guided treks to the peak. Krakauer made the ascent in 1996 as a reporter for *Outside Magazine* in what turned out to be the deadliest season on the mountain. His heart-pounding account covers the life and death stories of that awful season and the history of our fascination with Everest.

Mahoney, Rosemary

Down the Nile: Alone in a Fisherman's Skiff. 2007. Little, Brown and Co., ISBN 9780316107457, 273p. 📖.

The Nile has long exerted a fascination on travelers and Mahoney was no exception. She was determined to row a 120-mile stretch of the Nile between Aswan and Qena despite repeated warnings that a lone woman in Egypt could never do such a thing. She faced major challenges in obtaining a boat, evading police patrols, and avoiding harassment from predatory males. Along the way, she regales us with tales of earlier Nile travelers Florence Nightingale and Gustave Flaubert.

Polly, Matthew

American Shaolin: Flying Kicks, Buddhist Monks, and the Legend of the Iron Crotch: An Odyssey in the New China. 2007. Gotham Books, ISBN 9781592402625, 366p.

What motivated a self-described 98-pound Kansas weakling to travel to China and learn kung fu from the Shaolin Temple monks? Polly was determined to shed his nerdy self, willing to try almost anything to become a Shaolin warrior. In this lively account, he regales us with the brutal training regimen, the drinking bouts, the friendships, and his insights into China of the early 1990s.

Rinella, Steven

American Buffalo: In Search of a Lost Icon. 2008. Spiegel & Grau, ISBN 9780385521680, 277p.

When Rinella literally stumbled over a buffalo skull in Alaska, he became fascinated with the animal, traveling miles to learn about its 40,000-year history. In 2005 he received one of the few permits granted by Alaska to hunt buffalo along the Copper River. Rinella interweaves his story of that hunt with his quest to learn about the magnificent animal that once populated the West.

Salak, Kira

The Cruelest Journey: Six Hundred Miles to Timbuktu. 2005. National Geographic Society, ISBN 9780792274575, 229p.

Salak, at 32, challenged herself to the limit: she kayaked alone 600 miles down the Niger River to the ancient city of Timbuktu, following the path of the Scottish explorer Mungo Park. Parts of the river are still just as Park would have seen them 200 years ago and Salak coped with the some of the same problems: hippos, tropical storms, dysentery, and campsites in places of doubtful safety. Her account is filled with determination and exhilaration at the sense of freedom and accomplishment that comes from pushing limits.

Pet Projects: The Animals in Our Lives

Animals star in these touching, humorous, and sometimes redemptive memoirs. Besides the usual cats and dogs, a horse, a pig, and several other charismatic animals make appearances, gracing humans with their wisdom and compassion.

Bernikow, Louise
Bark If You Love Me: A Woman-Meets-Dog Story. 2000. Algonquin Books of Chapel Hill, ISBN 1565122585, 206p.

    Bernikow lived on the Upper West Side of Manhattan, an independent city dweller, whose vision of life certainly did not include a dog. Then there was Libro, an abandoned boxer with a limp but with exceptional joie de vivre. From Libro's generosity of spirit, Bernikow learned lessons about unconditional love, courage, and flexibility that changed her life.

Grogan, John
Marley & Me: Life and Love with the World's Worst Dog. 2005. Wm. Morrow, ISBN 0060817089, 291p.

    Grogan and his wife decided that a dog would help them learn parenting skills before they had children, but they were unprepared for good-natured, independent Marley, the yellow lab whose energy couldn't be tamed. Marley was thrown out of obedience school, regularly ate through the garage door, and swallowed just about anything he could find. The Grogans' adventures with Marley and their own family struggles make an engaging, heartfelt, and often comical story. The book was made into a film and Grogan has written a second memoir about growing up and away from his parents called *The Longest Trip Home.*

Katz, Jon
Dog Days: Dispatches from Bedlam Farm. 2007. Villard, ISBN 9781400064045, 273p.

    Katz's warmhearted memoir of the good life in upstate New York is filled with the adventures and personalities of his animals, insights into the human-animal bond, and how he attempts to live in harmony with nature. His beloved dogs are joined by sheep, cows, donkeys, and chickens in this paean to country life which will enchant those longing to escape from city life and delight fans of his earlier books, including *A Dog Year* and *The Dogs of Bedlam Farm.*

Kerasote, Ted

Merle's Door: Lessons from a Freethinking Dog. 2007. Harcourt, ISBN 9780151012701, 398p.

   Merle turned up one day and nature-writer Kerasote was hooked; he took Merle home to Wyoming and so began a 13-year partnership with a dog of unusual intelligence and abilities. Kerasote let Merle develop a life of his own, coming and going through his own door, choosing when he ate. Along with wonderful stories about Merle, Kerasote writes about research on canine behavior and the canine-human bond.

Montgomery, Sy

⇨ *The Good Good Pig: The Extraordinary Life of Christopher Hogwood.* 2006. Ballantine Books, ISBN 9780345481375, 228p. 📖.

   Christopher Hogwood was a sickly piglet when Montgomery and her husband took him home, nursed him, and discovered his special brand of sociability. Montgomery, a nature writer and activist who preferred animals to people, found that Chris's ability to attract friends brought warmth and community to her life in unexpected and special ways.

Morris, Willie

My Cat Spit McGee. 1999. Random House, ISBN 0375503218, 141p.

   Morris grew up in the South, where dogs were his companions; cats had no place in his world. The challenge came with his second wife, a cat lover, and the white kitten, named Spit, who was born with Morris's help. Spit had one blue and one golden eye, slept with all four legs straight up, and generally proved to be an eccentric and lovable companion. Morris charts his growing attachment to Spit and muses on the universals of cat behavior. Readers may also enjoy Morris's memoir *My Dog Skip* or his classic memoir of childhood and young adulthood *North Toward Home.*

Myron, Vicki, with Brett Witter

Dewey: The Small-Town Library Cat Who Touched the World. 2008. Grand Central Publishing, ISBN 9780446407410, 277p. 📖.

   Myron, director of the Spencer Public Library in northwestern Iowa, found a shivering kitten in the book drop one cold January morning in 1988. Myron tells how Dewey, with his warm and loving nature, cheered up a town in crisis and helped Myron navigate through her own medical and family problems.

Tarte, Bob
Enslaved by Ducks: How One Man Went from Head of the Household to Bottom of the Pecking Order. 2003. Algonquin Books of Chapel Hill, ISBN 1565123514, 308p.

Although Tarte admits "you open up your heart to an animal at your peril," he and his wife Linda did just that to a menagerie of rabbits, cats, ducks, geese, turkeys, and parrots in their rural Michigan home. The tale of their first pet, Binky, the rabbit with attitude, starts off a string of hilarious and touching stories about pets with unusually exuberant and unnerving personalities.

Relativity: Unusual Family Experiences

Interesting family memoirs don't have to deal with extreme unhappiness or dysfunction. These memoirs take us on a search for family traditions, introduce unusual family members, and explore this most basic of relationships in some of its myriad varieties.

Apple, Max
Roommates: My Grandfather's Story. 1994. Warner Books, ISBN 0446518263, 211p.

Apple spins a captivating story of his relationship with his indomitable grandfather Rocky, a Lithuanian immigrant baker. When Apple went to graduate school, Rocky went with him as his 93-year-old roommate. Their loving but prickly relationship managed to survive the changing world of the 1960s, girlfriends, marriage, illness, and death. He also wrote a memoir about his grandmother: *I Love Gootie.*

Beck, Martha Nibley
Expecting Adam: A True Story of Birth, Rebirth, and Everyday Magic. 1999. Times Books, ISBN 0812929802, 328p. 📖.

Beck and her husband were at Harvard, working furiously on their graduate degrees, when Beck unexpectedly became pregnant with their second child. She felt immediately that something was different this time, but was unprepared for the out-of-body experiences and wonderful coincidences that saved her life and sanity. Adam, a Down syndrome child, turned their lives around in marvelous ways. Skeptics should be prepared to be won over by this charming, funny, and very spiritual memoir.

Brenner, Marie

Apples and Oranges: My Brother and Me, Lost and Found. 2008. Farrar, Straus and Giroux, ISBN 9780374173524, 268p. 📖.

Brenner and her brother were always at odds, with a relationship "like tangled fishing line." She became an investigative journalist in New York; he grew apples and pears in Washington State. Their politics, personalities, and lifestyles were miles apart and their relationship often acrimonious until he became ill and reached out to her. As Brenner came to understand the person her brother had become, they earned a hard-won reconciliation.

Haizlip, Shirlee Taylor

⇨ *The Sweeter the Juice: A Family Memoir in Black and White.* 1994. Simon & Schuster, ISBN 0671792350, 271p. 📖.

Haizlip examines the effects of race in America through her own family's tangled history of white, African American, and Native American roots. Some of her relatives lived as African Americans, some passed as whites, splitting siblings apart and separating parents and children by reason of skin tone and hair texture. Haizlip searched and found relatives long missing from family gatherings, revealing the truly complex story of American identity.

Lagnado, Lucette

The Man in the White Sharkskin Suit: My Family's Exodus from Old Cairo to the New World. 2007. Ecco Press, ISBN 9780060822125, 340p. 📖.

Lagnado grew up in Cairo in the 1950s, the youngest of four siblings and her father Leon's favorite. He was a charismatic, self-absorbed Jewish boulevardier, who neglected his family for Cairo's heady night life. When the family had to flee the country in 1963, the children were able to make the transition, but it was too difficult for Leon. Lagnado vividly evokes the rich cultural stew of Cairo, making the contrast with their dispiriting life in Brooklyn all the more haunting.

Li, Leslie

Daughter of Heaven: A Memoir with Earthly Recipes. 2005. Arcade Publishing, ISBN 1559707682, 274p.

Growing up Chinese American in New York, Li absorbed messages from two cultures and was often at odds with her traditional father. She was warmed by the cooking of her grandmother Nai-nai, who took over the sandbox to plant bok choy and offered, with her meals, a delicious link to her Chinese family. Li's literate prose is rich with descriptions of food and family relationships.

Schenone, Laura

The Lost Ravioli Recipes of Hoboken: A Search for Food and Family. 2008. W.W. Norton & Co., ISBN 9780393061468, 331p. 📖.

Schenone searched for her great-grandmother's Christmas ravioli recipe to recapture the taste of the past for a family far from their immigrant roots in Genoa, Italy, and Hoboken, New Jersey. As she learned the secrets of ravioli-making from cooks in Italy and long-lost relatives in the United States, she came to understand how food and love are intertwined in all our lives. Recipes included.

Suberman, Stella

The Jew Store. 1998. Algonquin Books of Chapel Hill, ISBN 1565121988, 298p. 📖.

In 1920, the Subermans arrived by horse and wagon in a small town in northwestern Tennessee to open a dry goods store. Local prejudices, Klan activity, and the absence of other Jewish families, made their adjustment difficult. By the time the family reluctantly left, 13 years later, the children had Southern accents and Southern friends, and the family and store had become part of the fabric of the town. This slice-of-life memoir recalls a Southern world long gone.

Rooting Around: Searching for Family Origins

The impulse to learn about our forebears is strong—who are we, where do we come from, why do our families behave the way they do? These authors were curious and followed their hearts to find answers and unlock secret histories.

Broyard, Bliss

One Drop: A True Story of Family, Race, and Secrets. 2007. Little, Brown and Co., ISBN 9780316163507, 514p. 📖.

Broyard grew up as the privileged daughter of the successful writer and literary critic Anatole Broyard. It was only on her father's deathbed that he revealed the family secret—he had passed as white. This revelation sent Broyard off on a search for lost family members in an attempt to understand her father's choices. In the process, we gain insight into the personal cost of racial politics.

Dubner, Stephen J.

⇨ *Turbulent Souls: A Catholic Son's Return to His Jewish Family.* 1998. William Morrow, ISBN 0688151809, 320p. 📖.

Dubner's parents, raised in observant Jewish families, found their separate ways to Catholicism, then found each other. Disowned by most of their relatives, they raised eight children and remained devout Catholics. Their youngest son, curious about the religion his parents rejected, embarked on a literal and spiritual journey to understand his parents' choices and find his own path.

Epstein, Helen

Where She Came From: A Daughter's Search for Her Mother's History. 1997. Little, Brown and Co., ISBN 0316246085, 322p.

Sparked by a desire to understand her mother's family history, Epstein traveled to Czechoslovakia, where she pieced together the life stories of her female relatives from the mid-19th century through the Holocaust. She discovered a remarkable group of capable independent women who had vibrant, successful lives despite persecution and difficult personal circumstances. This is a well-researched memoir with the appeal of historical fiction.

Mendelsohn, Daniel

The Lost: A Search for Six of Six Million. 2006. HarperCollins, ISBN 9780060542979, 512p. AW. 📖.

Mendelsohn's childhood was shadowed by the ghosts of six relatives killed in the Holocaust; no one knew how they died. He was intrigued by family letters and photographs and visited his family's home town of Bolechow to learn what happened to them. In this exhaustive, ruminative account of family members living and dead, Mendelsohn recalls the precise feeling of a grandmother's papery cheek and the way other people's memories can change our lives.

Pham, Andrew X.

Catfish and Mandala: A Two-Wheeled Voyage Through the Landscape and Memory of Vietnam. 1999. Farrar, Straus and Giroux, ISBN 0312267177, 344p. 📖.

Pham takes a literal and metaphorical trip through the ambiguous legacy of the Vietnam War. His family escaped in 1977 when he was 10, but the demons they brought with them to America played havoc with their lives. After his sister's suicide, Pham bicycled around Vietnam on a painful search for a sense of home. He brilliantly evokes the sights, sounds, smells, and tastes of Vietnam today. In a second family memoir, *The Eaves of Heaven: A Life in Three Wars,* he returns to Vietnam to search out his father's past.

Sabar, Ariel
My Father's Paradise: A Son's Search for his Jewish Past in Kurdish Iraq. 2008. Algonquin Books of Chapel Hill, ISBN 9781565124905, 352p. AW. 📖.

As a child, Sabar couldn't relate to his father, a Kurdish Jew and distinguished UCLA professor of Aramaic, but once he became a father himself, he wanted to learn his own history. He traveled to Zakho in Iraq, the remote Kurdish village where his father was born, then followed in his father's footsteps to Israel. In bringing us this account of a little-known chapter in modern Jewish history, Sabar combines a personal story with insights into a very troubled part of the world.

Tracey, Patrick Austin
Stalking Irish Madness: Searching for the Roots of My Family's Schizophrenia. 2008. Bantam Dell, ISBN 9780553805253, 273p. 📖.

Schizophrenia runs in Tracey's Irish family like a bad seed; his grandmother, uncle and two of his four sisters were afflicted. In an effort to understand the awful legacy, he traveled to Ireland, weaving together his family's sad history, the folklore of madness, and medical research into a narrative of hope and loss.

Sports Talk

These memoirs provide the adrenaline rush that comes from rooting for a team or a player and give us the inside track on the day-to-day details of a sport. The authors are passionate athletes and don't spare us the good, the bad, or the ugly.

Bouton, Jim
Ball Four: My Life and Hard Times Throwing the Knuckleball in the Big Leagues. 1990 (1970). Collier Books, ISBN 0025139800, 472p.

Former Major League pitcher Bouton's memoir of his 1969 season was an eye opener for baseball fans who preferred to think of their heroes—like Mickey Mantle—as clean cut aw-shucks guys. Bouton was reviled by players, coaches, and sportswriters for revealing the extent of obscene language, petty behavior, womanizing, and drug and alcohol abuse among the players. Notoriety aside, it's a fascinating look at one season from the vantage point of the pitcher's mound.

Bruschi, Tedy, with Michael Holley

Never Give Up: My Stroke, My Recovery and My Return to the NFL. 2007. Wiley, ISBN 9780470108697, 268p.

In February 2005, everything was going well for Boston Patriots linebacker Tedy Bruschi: the Patriots had won their third Superbowl, he was the proud father of three sons, and he was one of the most popular players with teammates and fans. No one could have predicted the stroke that would sideline him, affecting his coordination, vision, and heart. His road back to football after only eight months is an inspiring and courageous tale of determination and drive.

Coyne, Tom

A Course Called Ireland: A Long Walk in Search of a Country, a Pint, and the Next Tee. 2009. Gotham Books, ISBN 9781592404247, 311p.

Coyne had fond memories of a golfing trip he took to Ireland with his Dad when he was 19. Now at age 30, with parenthood looming, he set himself a golfing challenge: to circumnavigate Ireland—on foot—and play almost 60 courses. Toting his clubs and a backpack, for 16 weeks he trekked happily from town to town, from B&B to golf course to pub, making friends, eating and drinking too much, and sharing his insights on golf, Ireland, and blisters.

Dundee, Angelo, with Bert Sugar

My View from the Corner: A Life in Boxing. 2008. McGraw Hill, ISBN 9780071477390, 327p.

Legendary trainer of Muhammad Ali and other great fighters, Dundee was in the corner for some of the classic title bouts: Ali vs. Liston, Ali vs. Foreman, Leonard vs. Duran. He shares his insider's view of the fighters' colorful personalities, sparing none of the drama. Have you ever wanted to know what happens between a trainer and a boxer in the 60 seconds between rounds? This lively memoir provides a ringside seat.

Fatsis, Stefan

A Few Seconds of Panic: A 5-Foot-8, 43-Year-Old Sportswriter Plays in the NFL. 2008. Penguin Press, ISBN 9781594201783, 340p.

Fatsis lived the dream of many sports fans: he spent three months as a place-kicker with the Denver Broncos in an effort to understand the rigors and culture of his favorite sport. Training and living with the players, he coped with aging knees and public failure as he attempted to hone his skills and become accepted by the team. Fun and fascinating participatory journalism in the footsteps of the late George Plimpton.

Jericho, Chris, with Peter Thomas Fornatale
  A Lion's Tale: Around the World in Spandex. 2007. Warner Books, ISBN 9780446580069, 412p.

  By the age of eight, Jericho knew he wanted to be a wrestler like all those crazy larger-than-life guys he and his father watched and cheered for. He learned his chops in a tough Canadian wrestling school, fought in matches in Mexico and Japan, and in 1999 joined World Wrestling Entertainment. His rollicking story of people and events is filled with affection and humor.

Roy, Alexander
  The Driver: My Dangerous Pursuit of Speed and Truth in the Outlaw Racing World. 2007. HarperEntertainment, ISBN 9780061227936, 326p.

  On his deathbed, Roy's father revealed he had a secret life driving in illegal cross country road rallies. Tantalized by the stories, Roy entered this mysterious, high-risk, all-or-nothing world of speed freaks; he competed in rallies all over the world, winning the Gumball 3000 in 2006. Written at high speed, this is a colorful, riveting story.

Shirley, Paul
  ⇨ *Can I Keep My Jersey?: 11 Teams, 5 Countries, and 4 Years in My Life as a Basketball Vagabond.* 2007. Villard, ISBN 9780345491367, 326p.

  Shirley's four-year diary of his life on the court comes from his ESPN blog My So-Called Career. As a good but not star player, he's been on six NBA teams, played in Spain and Greece, and in the minor leagues. With a detached, ironic, and self-deprecating tone, he reports on his life with a very select group of athletes.

Under Fire: Stories of War

The violence of combat has left its mark on all these authors: their memoirs are intensely personal, filled with graphic descriptions and raw emotions. We read their stories to share their experiences and understand history from a very personal point of view.

Brittain, Vera

Testament of Youth: An Autobiographical Study of the Years 1900–1925. 2005 (1933). Penguin Books, ISBN 0143039237, 661p. 📖.

The impact of World War I on English women has never been better portrayed than in this memoir, a classic in England. Vera Brittain's traditional middle-class life was shattered when her fiancé and brother were both killed in combat. She abandoned college and her "provincial young-ladyhood" and volunteered for nurse training, serving in Malta and France. Her wartime experiences are graphically detailed in this story of loss and shattered ideals.

Campbell, Donovan

Joker One: A Marine Platoon's Story of Courage, Leadership, and Brotherhood. 2009. Random House, ISBN 9781400067732, 313p.

As a marine lieutenant, Campbell spent most of 2004 in the city of Ramadi, Iraq, with his 40-man infantry platoon, in unrelenting counterinsurgency battles with an enemy almost impossible to distinguish from the civilian population. He briefly tells how he never intended to join the Marines, and only did so for the challenge of leadership, but the real story is about the men he fought with: their bravery, comradeship, loyalty, and support of each other. He brings to life the texture of their daily lives in that perilous time.

Caputo, Philip

⇨ *A Rumor of War.* 1996 (1977). Henry Holt, ISBN 9780805046953, 356p. AW. 📖.

Caputo arrived in Vietnam with the first marine troops in 1965 and his experiences were emblematic of all that followed: the frustrations of fighting a rarely seen enemy in hostile jungle terrain and the difficulty of differentiating civilians from Viet Cong. His descriptions of the moral ambiguity of the war, the way 19-year-olds were turned into angry killers, and the "nameless numbered hills and joyless, raining dawns" have made this a wartime classic. Readers will find themselves gripped by the visceral way he recalls the soldier's life.

Hynes, Samuel

Flights of Passage: Reflections of a World War II Aviator. 2003 (1988). Penguin Books, ISBN 0142002909, 270p.

Hynes's nostalgic memoir of his time training as a pilot and flying bombers in the South Pacific is as much about being very young and untried as it is about World War II. As he trained in various locations, he became close friends with a diverse group of young men, met his future wife, and learned about death. For some readers his story will recall a familiar time past; for others, it will bring the 1940s to life.

Jadick, Richard, with Thomas Hayden
   On Call in Hell: A Doctor's Iraq War Story. 2007. NAL Caliber (Penguin), ISBN 9780451220530, 275p.
      At the age of 38, Jadick left his wife and newborn baby and volunteered as a doctor in Iraq to fulfill a dream of serving in combat with the Marines. As battalion senior medical officer during the Battle of Fallujah, he set up a medical station in the thick of the fighting so marines could be treated faster. His account is gripping and bloody, filled with remarkable tales of heroism.

Kovic, Ron
   Born on the Fourth of July. 2005 (1976). Akashic Books, ISBN 9781888451788, 216p. AW
      Growing up, Kovic's heroes were John Wayne and Audie Murphy, so it seemed natural after high school to enlist in the Marines and fight in Vietnam, but during his second tour of duty he was shot and paralyzed from the chest down. Dismayed by the poor conditions he saw at VA hospitals, he began attending protests and demonstrations and became one of the most visible members of Vietnam Veterans Against the War. The unpretentious, deeply felt story of his journey from innocence to experience has become a classic, and was the basis of a movie by the same name.

Loyd, Anthony
   My War Gone By, I Miss it So. 1999. Atlantic Monthly Press, ISBN 0871137690, 321p.
      Loyd arrived in Bosnia in 1993, looking for a conflict that would quiet the demons that had driven him to drug abuse and depression. In the ghastly battles that pitted Serbs, Croatians, and Bosnian Muslims against each other, he found a calling as a journalist, going deep into the conflict with little thought for his own safety. This is graphic stuff, not for the fainthearted.

O'Brien, Tim
   If I Die in a Combat Zone: Box Me Up and Ship Me Home. 1999 (1973). Broadway Books, ISBN 0767904435, 209p. 📖.
      With his title, O'Brien summons up the mixture of fear, boredom, and desperation that characterized the soldier's life in the Vietnam War. O'Brien

allowed himself to be drafted after college, but with his strong anti-war beliefs he came close to deserting during training. His graphic, literate writing in this deeply personal memoir brings to life the harrowing experience of the foot soldier in combat. He is also the author of the acclaimed war novel, *Going After Cacciato*.

Chapter Three

Setting

Setting, as it's used here, isn't just geographical; it refers to memoirs that are rich in description—of time periods, places, milieus, professions, and intense experiences. Andre Aciman brings to life what it was like to grow up in Alexandria, Egypt, in the 1950s in *Out of Egypt.* We experience the Cultural Revolution in China with Da Chen in *Colors of the Mountain.* Ted Conover's memoir *Newjack* takes us inside the claustrophobic and scary world of a prison guard at Sing Sing. And with Sharon Osbourne, in *Extreme,* we share her frenetic life as music promoter and wife of Ozzy Osbourne. Of course, there are traditional travel memoirs in this chapter as well, so armchair travelers can roam the world or revisit places they've enjoyed.

There's also an educational aspect to many of these life stories. Readers often say that they like to learn something while they read for pleasure. The memoirs in this chapter provide a chance to learn from insiders: Michael Novacek on the world of the dinosaur hunter, in *Time Traveler: In Search of Dinosaurs and Ancient Mammals from Montana to Mongolia,* or Claire McCarthy on becoming a pediatrician, in *Learning How the Heart Beats: The Making of a Pediatrician.* Those autobiographies are rich in subject content about professions; other autobiographies teach us about what it was like in different times and places. Alexandra Fuller describes growing up in Africa at a time when colonialism was coming to an end in *Don't Let's Go to the Dogs Tonight.* Mildred Kalish recreates her Depression-era childhood on a farm in Iowa in *Little*

Heathens. A coal-mining town in the 1950s is the setting for Homer Hickam's vivid childhood memoir *Rocket Boys.*

We may not learn as much about the history and personality of the author as we would in character-intensive life stories, but we've shared an important, often significant part of their lives. And these books offer one of the great joys of reading life stories: the authors reflect on how their experiences changed them or deepened their understanding of the world and their fellow human beings. There are rich rewards here for all readers.

Eureka! Scientists at Work

These scientists are all passionate about the work that they do and want to share it with us. There's plenty of information here, but also the personal experiences that led the authors to their chosen fields.

Collet, Anne, with Marc Sich, trans. by Gayle Wurst
Swimming with Giants: My Encounters with Whales, Dolphins, and Seals.
2000. Milkweed Editions, ISBN 1571312447, 221p.

    Collet, founder and director of the Center for Research on Marine Mammals in La Rochelle, France, writes about her experiences studying whales and dolphins. A childhood fascination with the sea and an encounter with a friendly dolphin led to her career. We travel with her to Argentina, where a whale offers her a ride, and to the Arctic and the Azores, on whale counting expeditions, sharing her passionate advocacy for marine mammals in this blend of memoir and science.

Feynman, Richard P., as told to Ralph Leighton
"Surely You're Joking, Mr. Feynman!": Adventures of a Curious Character.
1985. W.W. Norton & Co., ISBN 0393019217, 350p.

    The brilliant physicist who exposed the shuttle O-ring failure with a glass of water, writes about the subjects that have interested his intensely curious mind, from the behavior of ants to our sense of smell. He fixed neighbors' radios as a child in Depression-era Brooklyn and worked for the Manhattan Project when barely out of Princeton University. Feynman's penchant for hilarious practical jokes enlivens these vignettes from a most unusual life. A companion volume, *What Do You Care What Other People Think?*, relates further adventures.

Novacek, Michael

Time Traveler: In Search of Dinosaurs and Ancient Mammals from Montana to Mongolia. 2002. Farrar, Straus and Giroux, ISBN 0374278806, 365p.

Like many children, Novacek was fascinated by dinosaurs and often visited La Brea Tar Pits near his home in Los Angeles, hoping to find fossils there and in his backyard. As an undergraduate at UCLA he was an indifferent student until he spent a summer in the deserts of Arizona and New Mexico, cracking open rocks to find fossils and learning the discipline of fieldwork. His memoir is chock full of information about paleontology and the joy of discovery, a rich find for anyone who has ever wondered about dinosaurs.

Owens, Mark, and Delia Owens

Cry of the Kalahari. 1984. Houghton Mifflin, ISBN 0395322146, 341p.

Mark and Delia Owens met as undergraduate biology majors, drawn together by their love of wild places. Together they pooled their meager resources and moved to Deception Valley in Africa's Kalahari Desert, one of the loneliest and most inhospitable landscapes imaginable. They lived there in a makeshift camp for seven years studying the wildlife, while coping with drought, fire, and lack of every convenience. Theirs is an exhilarating story of persistence and resourcefulness.

Pepperberg, Irene M.

⇨ *Alex and Me: How a Scientist and a Parrot Discovered a Hidden World of Animal Intelligence—And Formed a Deep Bond in the Process.* 2008. Collins, ISBN 9780061672477, 232p. 📖.

Pepperberg, a professor of animal cognition, writes engagingly about her work and relationship with Alex, an African Grey parrot with remarkable abilities and personality. Despite a brain "the size of a shelled walnut," Alex learned words and used them with intention and understood concepts of size and quantity, challenging the boundaries of avian intelligence. Pepperberg often struggled for recognition of her research but never doubted its value. Alex was her loving companion and collaborator; by the time of his death in 2007, he was an international celebrity, too.

Sapolsky, Robert M.

A Primate's Memoir. 2001. Scribner, ISBN 0743202473, 304p.

Fascinated by the dioramas at the Museum of Natural History in New York, Sapolsky wanted to be a mountain gorilla when he grew up; ultimately his research on primates took him to Africa to live with a baboon troop and study stress-related disease. Fresh out of Harvard, only 21, he worked hard to learn the skills he needed and get along with the neighboring warlike Masai tribe. Totally accessible to the general reader, Sapolsky's account of his life with the baboons is witty, informative, and utterly delightful.

Watson, James D.
   The Double Helix: A Personal Account of the Discovery of the Structure of DNA. 1998 (1968). Scribner, ISBN 0684852799, 226p. ██. ▢.
   Watson and Crick's discovery of the structure of DNA in 1953 revolutionized the field of biogenetics and brought them the Nobel Prize. Here Watson concentrates on the human side of the story: the excitement of scientific discovery, the foibles of the very human cast of characters involved, and the competitive nature of high-stakes research. Accessible and very opinionated, he offers a unique look into a rarefied world.

Far Out: Travel to Unusual Places

Wild, untamed places call out to these adventurous souls; they're motivated by wanderlust and find daily life a bore. These travel narratives offer a chance to learn about places that are not on the usual tourist itineraries.

Grant, Richard
   God's Middle Finger: Into the Lawless Heart of the Sierra Madre. 2008. Free Press, ISBN 9781416534402, 288p.
   Grant offers a compulsively readable account of his travels in the scenic mountains of western Mexico where tense encounters with trigger-happy drug runners, bandits, and corrupt police satisfied his craving for adventure. He also met up with more benign locals who filled him in on the area's long outlaw traditions. Along the way he—and the reader—acquire an extensive vocabulary of Spanish obscenities.

Newby, Eric
   A Short Walk in the Hindu Kush. 2005 (1959). Lonely Planet Publications, ISBN 0864426046, 255p.
   In this very British travel adventure, Newby, fed up with his fashion industry job, invited his old friend Hugh Carless on a trek to the Hindu Kush. After a four-day rock-climbing tutorial they set off for this very wild and beautiful area of Afghanistan to climb 19,000-foot Mir Samir. Newby's very droll

account of how these amateur adventurers, pipes in hand, managed to succeed in their quest, is a classic of travel writing.

O'Hanlon, Redmond

In Trouble Again: A Journey Between the Orinoco and the Amazon. 1989. Atlantic Monthly Press, ISBN 0871132494, 272p.

O'Hanlon ventures where no overweight, unfit British traveler should go; this time the passionate naturalist travels deep into the Venezuelan Amazon hoping to encounter the fierce Yanomami tribe. With his unique dry wit and enthusiasm for ingesting every new substance he encounters, he takes us through the beautiful and dangerous landscape, sightings of magnificent bird and animal life, and lunches of smoked tapir and piranha.

O'Hanlon, Redmond

➪ *Into the Heart of Borneo.* 1985. Random House, ISBN 0394544811, 191p.

O'Hanlon's rollicking account of his journey through the jungles of Borneo, into areas not explored since 1926, is a delightful armchair travel experience. Ostensibly motivated by a desire to find the rarely seen Borneo rhino, O'Hanlon and his friend, the poet James Fenton, light out with three native Iban guides into leech- and parasite-infested territory. The humor—and the author—are quintessentially, dryly British.

Shah, Tahir

In Search of King Solomon's Mines. 2002. Arcade Publishing, ISBN 1559706414, 240p.

In the Jerusalem souk, Shah buys a treasure map that marks the location of King Solomon's mines and he's off on a quest for the fabled source of the gold that was used to build the Holy Temple. He heads for Addis Ababa and joins forces with Samson, his Bible-reading guide; together they travel around Ethiopia by dilapidated bus, train, taxi, and mule, visiting the hyena-man of Harar, the castles of Gondar, the mountain of Tullu Wallel, and other strange and out-of-the-way places in this rollicking search for the ancient mines.

Stewart, Rory

The Places in Between. 2006. Harcourt, ISBN 9780156031561, 299p.

In January 2002, only two months after the Taliban were ousted, Stewart hiked across mountainous central Afghanistan from Herat to Kabul, part of a larger trek across Asia. Sleeping in rough mud huts and mosques, eating mostly bread and rice, and accompanied by an aging dog, he navigated literal and political minefields, treacherous winter conditions, and suspicious locals. It is an eye-opening account of the people and the countryside from a passionate and fearless traveler.

Thayer, Helen
Walking the Gobi: A 1600 Mile Trek across a Desert of Hope and Despair. 2007. The Mountaineers Books, ISBN 9781594850646, 251p.

At age 63, Thayer fulfilled a childhood dream and trekked 1,500 miles across the Gobi Desert in Mongolia accompanied by her 74-year-old husband and two camels. In furnace-like temperatures they braved sandstorms, stinging scorpions, loss of water, and officious Chinese border guards, reveling in the wild scenery and enjoying the hospitality of Mongolian nomads. Thayer's descriptions of their experiences are riveting and her determination is inspirational.

Thubron, Colin
Shadow of the Silk Road. 2007. HarperCollins, ISBN 9780061231728, 363p.

The Silk Road was an ancient trading route, bustling with markets and caravans, facilitating the flow of silk, spices, fabrics, and information from China to the Mediterranean. Thubron traveled the route, from Sian, in China, across Central Asia to Turkey, some 7,000 miles in eight months, riding third-class in trains, on buses and trucks, and talking to locals wherever he went. He describes the rich mixture of cultures, ethnicities, and religions that make this region perennially fascinating.

Wheeler, Sara
Terra Incognita: Travels in Antarctica. 1996. Random House, ISBN 9780679440789, 351p.

Wheeler thought of Antarctica as "a testing ground for men with frozen beards," but when she glimpsed it at the end of a trip to southern Chile, she was hooked, just like the great South Pole explorers Scott and Amundsen. She returned as a writer with a National Science Foundation team and penned this lively account of how scientists from various countries lived in this place of great beauty and great extremes.

Foreign Exchange: Encountering Other Cultures

One of the great pleasures of travel is spending time in another culture, trading the life you've been living for something different, even if it's only for a while. That's what motivated these authors to travel and report back to us on the sights, sounds, smells, and customs they encountered and reflect on how travel changed their lives.

Cohan, Tony
 On Mexican Time: A New Life in San Miguel. 2000. Broadway Books, ISBN 0767903188, 289p.

  Novelist Cohan and his wife Masako, tired of the frantic pace of their life in Los Angeles "hurtling down freeways toward receding destinations of evaporating worth," spent a few weeks in the Mexican hill town of San Miguel Allende. They were beguiled by the relaxed pace, the warmth of the people, the bright colors, enchanting flavors, and colorful fiestas. Impulsively, they sold their Los Angeles home and went to live in Mexico. Cohan's wonderful descriptions bring the town and its residents to life; we understand why they feel they've found paradise.

de Blasi, Marlena
 The Lady in the Palazzo: At Home in Umbria. 2006. Algonquin Books of Chapel Hill, ISBN 9781565124738, 317p.

  De Blasi's memoir is a feast of food and friendship, with recipes included, set in Orvieto, an ancient Italian hill town. While waiting for the renovations on their dilapidated medieval palazzo, de Blasi used her considerable cooking skills to win the friendship of her neighbors and become part of their lives. This memoir followed two others on living in Venice and Tuscany.

Doerr, Anthony
 Four Seasons in Rome: On Twins, Insomnia, and the Biggest Funeral in the History of the World. 2007. Scribner, ISBN 9781416540014, 210p.

  Doerr received a one year writing fellowship in Rome on the day his wife gave birth to twins; they packed up and moved from Idaho to an apartment near the Vatican with three-month-old Owen and Henry in tow. In his writing studio, Doerr found his novel-writing was stalled, taken over in the most delightful ways by the pleasures of Rome: people, art, street life, history, and culture. For anyone who has been to Rome or dreamt about going, this is a magical memoir.

Gelman, Rita Golden
 Tales of a Female Nomad: Living Large in the World. 2001. Crown Publishers, ISBN 0609606425, 311p. 📖.

  When Gelman's children went off to college, she and her husband realized they had little in common. She took a deep breath, went off to Mexico alone,

and discovered the joys of adventurous, serendipitous travel. Since then she
has lived with no fixed address, traveling around the world as a participant in
cultures from Indonesia to Israel to Guatemala. For anyone who has yearned to
step off the beaten tourist path, her story is inspirational.

Gopnik, Adam
⇨ *Paris to the Moon.* 2000. Random House, ISBN 0679444920, 338p.

French food and culture are on the menu in Gopnik's account of spending five years in Paris with his wife and small son, while on assignment for
The New Yorker magazine. Tempted by the beauty and glamour of Paris, they
were eager to raise a child whose playground was the Luxembourg Gardens
and who could absorb Parisian style from an early age. Learning to become
parents and learning about France are parallel journeys in this funny, tender,
and insightful memoir.

Horwitz, Tony
Baghdad without a Map, and Other Misadventures in Arabia. 1991. Dutton,
ISBN 0525249605, 285p.

Before the first Gulf War, journalist Horwitz traveled through 14 Middle
Eastern countries, reporting on stories for various publications. This collection
focuses in on the conversations he had with people in the street: merchants,
taxi drivers, soldiers, and government officials, as he tried to divide the personal from the political. Horwitz, a fearless and intrepid traveler, gives us the
fascinating back story to the current conflicts in the area.

Kapuscinski, Ryszard, trans. by Klara Glowczewska
Travels with Herodotus. 2007. Alfred A. Knopf, ISBN 9781400043385, 275p.

As a young journalist in mid-1950s Poland, Kapuscinski wanted to cross
borders and immerse himself in the life and culture of other countries. He
writes of his trips through India, the Far East, Middle East, and Africa, toting
a copy of Herodotus's *Histories,* which he relied on for insight into the nature
of travel and reportage. Always elegant and insightful, Kapuscinski is a great
traveling companion.

Mayes, Frances
Under the Tuscan Sun: At Home in Italy. 1996. Chronicle Books, ISBN
0811808424, 280p. 📖.

For several years, Mayes and her husband Ed searched Tuscany for a house
to buy. Nothing was right until they saw Bramasole in the town of Cortona,

a three-story, crumbling stone villa set in an olive orchard. Summer by summer, they lovingly renovated and restored, working with local artisans and learning the ways of the village. Her pleasure at their good fortune shines with the warmth of the Tuscan sun. Recipes included. Mayes has two more Tuscan memoirs: *Bella Tuscany* and *In Tuscany*.

Mitchell, John Hanson

The Rose Café: Love and War in Corsica. 2007. Shoemaker & Hoard, ISBN 9781593760953, 243p.

In 1962 Mitchell was a bored American student in Paris who took a casual trip to Corsica and found a place to write at the Rose Café. He stayed on, fascinated by Corsica's shadowy history and its magical, rugged landscape. With effortless elegance, he recalls the spell of Corsica's languid pace, the World War II stories of the locals who took refuge there, and how, in that nurturing setting, his own writing began to flourish.

Sachs, Dana

The House on Dream Street: Memoir of an American Woman in Vietnam. 2000. Algonquin Books of Chapel Hill, ISBN 1565122917, 348p.

Journalist Sachs was too young to remember the Vietnam War, but old enough to be curious about our former enemies. During a trip to Vietnam in 1990, she felt certain that some part of her life was meant to be lived there. A few years later she returned to Hanoi, where she spent a complicated year trying to understand and fit into a culture in the midst of reinventing itself. For fans of *Eat, Pray, Love,* this is another engaging seeker's tale.

Stewart, Chris

Driving Over Lemons: An Optimist in Andalucia. 1999. Pantheon, ISBN 0375410287, 248p.

Stewart, a sheep shearer and former Genesis drummer, and his wife Ana, quit England for a ramshackle farm in the hills of Andalucia, Spain, in this charming and gently humorous romp. Their new house lacked electricity, running water, a sound roof, and an access road, but they worked hard at improving their little paradise, learning the customs of their working-class farming region and which neighbors they could trust for help and advice. Much local wine is consumed in the process, sheep are safely sheared, and a baby girl is born.

A Hard Day's Night: Life in the Music Business

They've seen it all and lived large! These memoirs are often candid in the extreme; they capture a world of fame and excess far removed from most of our lives—that's what makes them so much fun to read.

Cash, Johnny, with Patrick Carr

Cash: The Autobiography. 1997. HarperSanFrancisco, ISBN 0062515004, 310p.

At the age of 65, Cash wrote this modest autobiography looking back on the highs and lows of a life in the public eye. Although a country music legend, he was fired from the Grand Ole Opry; despite tremendous commercial success, he suffered from drug addiction and attempted to take his own life. He reveals why he always wears black, dispels some myths, and tells about the great musicians he's been fortunate to know.

Clapton, Eric

⇨ *Clapton: The Autobiography.* 2007. Broadway Books, ISBN 9780385518512, 343p.

Clapton's very candid autobiography starts out slowly, with his childhood and the events that shaped his personality, then shifts into high gear as he becomes a major player on the 1960s music scene. Despite acclaim, he lacked self-confidence and direction, and succumbed to the destructive drug-, alcohol-, and sex-fueled 1970s pop music lifestyle. Clapton knew and jammed with everyone of consequence; readers will enjoy his tales of playing with all the greats, from George Harrison to Muddy Waters.

Dunn, Jancee

But Enough About Me: A Jersey Girl's Unlikely Adventures Among the Absurdly Famous. 2006. HarperCollins, ISBN 9780060843649, 276p. 📖.

In this rollicking trip through the world of pop culture, Dunn tells how she grew up in suburban New Jersey, in the hedonistic, label-conscious 1980s, a hipster wannabe. After dropping out of college, she landed her dream job at *Rolling Stone* magazine and began to interview rock stars. Chapters about her life alternate with advice on interviewing the rich and famous—for example, why you should always bring breath mints when interviewing rock bands. Dunn is refreshingly honest about her interviewees but ambivalent about her time as a "rock chick."

Ian, Janis
Society's Child: My Autobiography. 2008. Jeremy P. Tarcher/Penguin, ISBN 9781585426751, 361p.

    Singer-songwriter Ian's childhood was cut short at age 15 with the success of her first recorded song, *Society's Child.* She quickly became a fixture on the folk music scene of the 1960s, but the pressures of the recording world were overwhelming for a teenager. Her candid memoir tells of years honing her craft while fighting illness, a bad marriage, and the IRS; she also brings to life the era when folk music ruled the airwaves.

Lindeen, Laurie
Petal Pusher: A Rock and Roll Cinderella Story. 2007. Atria Books, ISBN 9780743292320, 320p.

    Smart, funny, and wise, Lindeen recalls how she and two friends created the all-girl punk rock band Zuzu's Petals in Minneapolis in the 1980s. Lindeen, "a cranked-up new wave angel in elf boots" with a diagnosis of multiple sclerosis providing an urgent drumbeat, started with a cast-off guitar. She captures the road trips, the gigs good and bad, the drugs, boyfriends, fans, and the boredom that brought the band to an end.

Osbourne, Sharon, with Penelope Dening
Extreme: My Autobiography. 2006. St. Martin's Press, ISBN 9780821280140, 365p.

    From the beginning, Osbourne's life was filled with violence and music. Her memoir takes us on a roller coaster ride from childhood in Brixton, daughter of the cutthroat rock promoter Don Arden, to wife and manager of shock-rocker Ozzy Osbourne. It's a raunchy insider's tale, complete with the famous stories of Ozzy's outrageous behavior, their abusive drug- and alcohol-fueled lifestyle, and financial woes. Through it all, Sharon Osbourne floats with humor, tenacity, and burning love for Ozzy.

Slash, with Anthony Bozza
Slash. 2007. HarperEntertainment, ISBN 9780061351426, 457p.

    An entertaining, no-holds-barred life of the Guns N' Roses guitarist who grew up wild and free on the streets of Los Angeles, son of an African American clothing designer and a white British artist. Slash inherited his parents' artistry and love of literature; a chance meeting with a guitar gave him his own direction. He flew high with the band and its destructive sex-, drugs-, and alcohol-driven lifestyle, all recounted without apology or regret.

Life Support: Memoirs from the Medical World

These are powerful memoirs of life and death, opening a window for us into the way doctors and other health professionals make decisions and understand their profession.

Austin, Paul

⇨ *Something for the Pain: One Doctor's Account of Life and Death in the Emergency Room.* 2008. W.W. Norton & Co., ISBN 9780393065602, 297p.

Austin chose to specialize in Emergency Room medicine, fully aware that it would mean hectic, rotating shifts of crucial decision making but unprepared for the toll it would take on his psyche and his family. In recounting the stories of the patients he sees—the fevered child, the woman with the persistent headache, the violent drunks, and the attempted suicides—he describes the culture of the emergency room and his own efforts to find the balance between detachment and compassion that keeps his own life in balance.

Collins, Michael J.

Hot Lights, Cold Steel: Life, Death and Sleepless Nights in a Surgeon's First Years. 2005. St. Martin's Press, ISBN 0312337787, 308p.

Collins' account of his four years as an orthopedic resident at the Mayo Clinic hurtles along at breakneck speed, keeping pace with his experiences. He begins as an anxious newbie, certain he is "the dullest scalpel in the drawer," learning to treat physical injuries and their emotional consequences. During this time, Collins and his wife Patti have three children; to make ends meet he moonlights at another hospital, adding to his long shifts and sleep deprivation. Readers will be riveted by Collins's funny and vivid memoir.

Harman, Patricia

Blue Cotton Gown: A Midwife's Memoir. 2008. Beacon Press, ISBN 9780807072899, 290p. 📖.

Harman writes candidly about her life as a nurse-midwife in West Virginia and her patients: 17-year-old Heather, unmarried and pregnant with twins; Nila, estranged from her husband and pregnant with her eighth child; and Kasmar, a lesbian who wants help with a sex change. In the midst of her own financial, health, and marital problems, she struggles to offer not only medical advice and treatment, but support and understanding, telling heart-breaking stories with eloquence and insight.

McCarthy, Claire

Learning How the Heart Beats: The Making of a Pediatrician. 1995. Viking Press, ISBN 0670838748, 247p. 📖.

McCarthy knew from the time she was 12 that she wanted to be a pediatrician, but this Harvard-trained doctor wasn't prepared for how emotional it would be for her to treat sick children. It's also emotional for the reader as McCarthy tells how she learned about the human side of medicine by listening to her heart and her patients.

Siebert, Charles

A Man After His Own Heart: A True Story. 2004. Crown Publishers, ISBN 0609602217, 274p. 📖.

Siebert has a history of heartfelt concerns: his father died too young of heart disease and Siebert himself had several episodes of coronary neurosis, anxiety attacks centered on the workings of his heart. In this fascinating and lyrically written search to understand the physical and metaphysical nature of our hearts, he joins a transplant team and has the rare experience of touching a beating heart.

Trout, Nick

Tell Me Where it Hurts: A Day of Humor, Healing and Hope in my Life as an Animal Surgeon. 2008. Broadway Books, ISBN 9780767926430, 285p.

This 24-hour glimpse into the life of a staff surgeon in a large Boston veterinary hospital begins with a late night phone request to help a German shepherd in distress and continues through a long day of examinations, tricky diagnoses, surgeries, and consultations with distraught pet owners. Along the way, Trout takes time, with humor and empathy, to comment on issues of animal care, veterinary education, and the power of the relationship between man and beast.

Verghese, Abraham

My Own Country: A Doctor's Story of a Town and its People in the Age of AIDS. 1994. Simon & Schuster, ISBN 0671785141, 347p. 📖.

Verghese, an African Indian doctor at a rural Tennessee hospital in the mid-1980s, found that a growing number of gay men suffering from AIDS were coming home from the cities to die in their conservative hometowns. His decision to focus on their care, help them find social services, and deal with their shocked families changed his life. A moving elegy about the intersection of a doctor's practice with a devastating disease.

Orient Express: Travel to the Far East and Oceania

Although these travel memoirs are very different from each other, the authors all traveled with an intense desire to learn as much as they could about the people and places they visited. We benefit from their insights, whether their approach is lighthearted, serious, introspective, or adventurous.

Carey, Peter

Wrong About Japan: A Father's Journey with his Son. 2005. Alfred A. Knopf, ISBN 1400043115, 158p.

When novelist Carey's shy 12-year-old son Charley developed a love of manga and anime, Carey saw an opportunity for father-son bonding and took him to Japan. At interviews with manga artists and anime directors, he found that his preconceived ideas about Japanese culture were superficial or incorrect. Father and son learned about Japan and themselves in this candid and humorous account, enlivened by manga and anime illustrations.

Hessler, Peter

River Town: Two Years on the Yangtze. 2001. HarperCollins, ISBN 0060195444, 402p. AW. 📖.

In 1996, courtesy of the Peace Corps, Hessler arrived in the remote town of Fuling, where he taught English at a small teacher's college for two years. Situated along the Yangtze River and shortly to be changed forever by the Three Gorges Dam project, Fuling was a microcosm of the issues and contradictions of modern Chinese life. Hessler immersed himself in the culture and life of the college, teaching and learning; he shares the lessons he learned with wit and compassion.

Horwitz, Tony

Blue Latitudes: Boldly Going Where Captain Cook Has Gone Before. 2002. Henry Holt, ISBN 0805065415, 480p.

If James Cook's remarkable 18th-century voyages of discovery are just a dim schoolroom memory, Horwitz's fascinating travel memoir will bring you up to date. Cook's three voyages took him to many of the then exotic lands that touch the Pacific Ocean. Horwitz visits many of the same places: Hawaii, Tahiti, New Zealand, Australia, and the Pacific Northwest, where he contrasts his adventures with Cook's in this lively, entertaining romp.

Iyer, Pico
The Lady and the Monk: Four Seasons in Kyoto. 1992. Alfred A. Knopf, ISBN 0679403086, 337p. 📖.

On two brief visits to Japan, Iyer had an intense sense of belonging and returned in 1987 to spend a year in Kyoto and put the Japan of his imagination to the test. He anticipated a quiet, monk-like year, but soon met interesting expatriates and Japanese, especially the delightful Sachiko, mother of two young children, who opened her heart to Iyer. Filled with insight, warmth, and lyrical writing, Iyer's portrait of Japan is filled with rewards for the patient reader.

Theroux, Paul
The Great Railway Bazaar: By Train Through Asia. 2006 (1975). Houghton Mifflin, ISBN 9780618658947, 342p. AW.

This is armchair travel with an ideal companion on the famous railways of Asia and India: the Orient Express, the Khyber Mail, and the Trans-Siberian Express, among others, in search of intrigue, adventure, and enlightenment. Theroux's account is filled with wonderful turns of phrase; he's never at a loss in describing the colorful cultural landscape and reporting on the people he meets along the way. In 2008, Theroux retraced his steps and published an updated account, titled *Ghost Train to the Eastern Star: On the Tracks of the Great Railway Bazaar.*

Troost, J. Maarten
Getting Stoned with Savages: A Trip Through the Islands of Fiji and Vanuatu. 2006. Broadway Books, ISBN 9780767921992, 239p.

Two years of living in the South Pacific spoiled Troost for office life; when he was fired from his Washington D.C. office job, he and wife Sylvia happily jettisoned their furniture—and most of their clothing—to return. Life in Vanuatu and Fiji proved irresistible for Troost, who developed a fondness for drinking kava—a locally made intoxicant—with the natives. Troost's highly developed sense of irony permeates his hilarious adventures; the South Seas will never seem the same again. His earlier book about the South Pacific is *The Sex Lives of Cannibals: Adrift in the Equatorial Pacific.*

Troost, J. Maarten

Lost on Planet China: The Strange and True Story of One Man's Attempt to Understand the World's Most Mystifying Nation or How He Came to Love Live Squid. 2008. Broadway Books, ISBN 9780767922005, 382p.

Troost, author of hilarious travel memoirs about the South Pacific, offers his unique point of view on the largest—and most complex—country in the world. As he travels to cities like Beijing, Shanghai, and Hong Kong, to exotic Tibet, the Gobi Desert, and Shangri-La, he fills us in on China old and new. He sees fabulous skyscrapers and deformed beggars; learns to elbow his way through queues like everyone else; and does his best to avoid eating unusual animal body parts.

Warmbrunn, Erika

⇨ *Where the Pavement Ends: One Woman's Bicycle Trip Through Mongolia, China & Vietnam.* 2001. The Mountaineers Books, ISBN 0898866847, 249p.

Wherever she went on her 8,000-mile solo trip, people asked Warmbrunn if she was lonely or scared: she was neither. Instead, she reveled in the opportunity to explore wide open spaces and enjoyed the hospitality and friendship she found in villages off the beaten path. Her love of independent travel and her buoyant personality shine through in this remarkable memoir, which is absorbing from first to last page.

Wong, Jan

A Comrade Lost and Found: A Beijing Story. 2009. Houghton Mifflin Harcourt, ISBN 9780151013425, 322p. 📖.

In 1972, Wong was the first Canadian student to study in China. It was during the Cultural Revolution, and in her zeal for Maoism she reported a fellow student who had expressed a desire to visit the United States: Yin was denounced and expelled. Haunted by her unthinkable actions, Wong, now a journalist, returns to China years later with her husband and sons to see how the country has changed but also to try to locate Yin and make amends. Her poignant and informative memoir is part travel memoir and part personal journey.

Outside the Box: Interesting Occupations

This diverse group of authors write about the unusual jobs they've had and interesting career paths they've followed. Several of the authors never anticipated how casual choices would transform their lives.

Brazile, Donna
➪ *Cooking with Grease: Stirring the Pots in American Politics.* 2004. Simon & Schuster, ISBN 0743253981, 352p.

Brazile grew up in a poor, close-knit Louisiana family, where she learned the value of political activism starting at age nine. By her teens, she knew politics was her future. After college, she worked on several political campaigns, building her reputation as a gifted community organizer and a tireless, outspoken worker for African American civil rights and other causes. She was the campaign manager for the Gore-Lieberman ticket in 2000. Her remarkable story is filled with warmth and fascinating insider details.

Conover, Ted
Newjack: Guarding Sing Sing. 2000. Random House, ISBN 0375501770, 321p.

Journalist Conover was refused permission to profile a correctional officer recruit, so he went undercover and enrolled in the training program himself, spending a year as a "newjack" in New York's infamous Sing Sing prison. From boot camp style training to first days on the job, he learned the hard way about the dehumanizing, brutal aspects of prison life for inmates and guards and reported his experiences in this riveting, you-are-there account.

Fowler, Ruth
No Man's Land: A Memoir. 2008. Viking Press, ISBN 9780670019397, 265p.

Fowler left Cambridge University with a first-class degree but didn't follow the traditional path; she traveled, drank, and partied around Europe. At 25, in New York without a job or visa, she became "Mimi," a stripper in a sleazy club, anesthetized to the routine by alcohol. Fowler's lurid and sometimes stream-of-consciousness account of her year as a stripper is racy, literary, and very candid.

Goldsby, Robin Meloy
Piano Girl: Lessons in Life, Music, and the Perfect Blue Hawaiian. 2005. Backbeat Books, ISBN 0879308249, 278p.

Thirty years as a cocktail pianist have given Goldsby a trove of funny and touching stories about the foibles of drinkers, waiters, managers, stalkers, and musicians. She began playing in a Nantucket restaurant to earn college money but soon found jobs playing in fancy hotels and restaurants in interesting locations. Goldsby spikes her lively story with tongue-in-cheek advice and hard-won insights about human nature.

Greenlaw, Linda

The Hungry Ocean: A Swordboat Captain's Journey. 1999. Hyperion, ISBN 0786864516, 265p.

Greenlaw, the only female swordboat captain, spins a salty, descriptive yarn of a 30-day trip from Gloucester, Massachusetts, to the fishing grounds off Nova Scotia. She shares the hard work of preparing the equipment and keeping the crew focused, the drama of choosing the spot to fish, and the suspense of hauling in the catch. Along the way she writes about the culture of the fishing community and communicates her love of the sea-going life.

Lansky, Aaron

Outwitting History: The Amazing Adventures of a Man Who Rescued a Million Yiddish Books. 2004. Algonquin Books of Chapel Hill, ISBN 1565124294, 316p. AW. 📖.

Lansky took a Yiddish language course in college on a lark and discovered his mission: to save Yiddish books—and literature—from destruction as the last generation of Yiddish speakers died out. From collecting books with a truck and a few helpers, he established the National Yiddish Book Center, a vibrant cultural resource, and sparked a revival of Yiddish language and culture. A diverting, inspirational tale that proves that one person with a dream can make a difference.

Secrest, Meryle

Shoot the Widow: Adventures of a Biographer in Search of Her Subject. 2007. Alfred A. Knopf, ISBN 9780307264831, 242p. 📖.

A lively account of the ups and downs of writing about nine famous people, among them Salvador Dali, Stephen Sondheim, Frank Lloyd Wright, and Romaine Brooks. Secrest's pursuit of the inside story has required skills in empathy, diplomacy, and sleuthing: things aren't always what they seem. She also writes an engaging account of her life as a child in elegant Bath, England, and in Canada.

Shelton, Richard

Crossing the Yard: Thirty Years as a Prison Volunteer. 2007. University of Arizona Press, ISBN 9780816525942, 256p. 📖.

English professor Richard Shelton found such satisfaction in the creative writing classes he taught in the Arizona prison system that it became a 30-year commitment. Shelton fought the prejudices and ignorance of prison staff and persevered through riots and lockdowns to bring hope and education to inmates who became successful published writers and friends.

Stark, Tim
Heirloom: Notes from an American Tomato Farmer. 2008. Broadway Books, ISBN 9780767927062, 232p.

Stark was barely scraping by, a writer in a Brooklyn garret, when he built a germination rack for tomatoes from scavenged lumber. Those seedlings jumpstarted a business growing heirloom tomatoes on the Pennsylvania farm of his childhood. He learned the hard way about the vagaries of weather, insects, and employees; his charming memoir is filled with the satisfactions of bringing Black Krims and Zapotec Pleateds to our tables.

The Passing Scene: Road Trips

Haven't we all wanted at some time to cut loose from everyday life and take to the open road? Join these travelers as they explore back roads and interesting sights, cross borders, and take stock of their lives.

Bishop, Ted
Riding with Rilke: Reflections on Motorcycles and Books. 2006. W. W. Norton, ISBN 9780393062618, 261p.

English literature professor Bishop, on sabbatical from university, trades "tweed for leather" as he rides his Ducati from Alberta, Canada, to the University of Texas at Austin for research on Virginia Woolf. This unique and joyous paean to the riding and writing life is filled with tales about the small towns he visits and the pleasures of literary discovery.

Cahill, Tim
Road Fever: A High-Speed Travelogue. 1991. Random House, ISBN 039457656X, 278p.

Cahill, a founding editor of *Outside Magazine* and well-known for his unconventional travel reporting, drove from Tierra del Fuego at the tip of South America, to the Arctic Circle to claim the land speed record in 1987. Beef jerky, bad coffee, military checkpoints, and the hilarity of the seriously exhausted combine in this account of a riotous, marathon 24-day road trip. Cahill has published several collections of his travel essays, including *Hold the Enlightenment, Pass the Butterworms,* and *Jaguars Ripped My Flesh.*

Guevara, Ernesto (Che), trans. by Ann Wright

⇨ *The Motorcycle Diaries: A Journey Around South America.* 1995. Verso, ISBN 1859849423, 156p.

Guevara was a year short of finishing medical school when he and his friend Albert Granado took to the road on the sputtering, unreliable motorcycle they called La Poderosa II—the Mighty One. The account of their 8,000-mile trip through Argentina, Chile, Peru, Ecuador, Colombia, Venezuela, and Panama is filled with delight in the natural beauty and Guevara's growing understanding that his calling was not in the research lab but on the front lines of political and social change. The diary was made into a movie of the same name in 2004.

Hawks, Tony

Round Ireland with a Fridge. 2000. Thomas Dunne Books, ISBN 0312242360, 247p.

What was he thinking? Hawks bet a friend that he could hitchhike with a fridge around the circumference of Ireland in 30 days, and set off on a hilarious excursion filled with bizarre encounters—often in pubs—where the "Fridge Man" was welcomed as a curious celebrity. Along the way, the fridge went surfing and Hawks met an island king. Hawks took on another bet for his next book *Playing the Moldovans at Tennis.*

Henderson, Kristin

Driving by Moonlight: A Journey Through Love, War, and Infertility. 2003. Seal Press, ISBN 1580050980, 309p.

Henderson and husband Frank worked hard to overcome their differences: he was a Lutheran minister, she turned away from his religion; she wanted children, he didn't. When he left to serve as a chaplain in Afghanistan after 9/11, she took her old Corvette on a road trip. As she explored back roads, thought about her fertility problems, exchanged e-mail with Frank, and meditated about the consequences of the bombings, she began to let go of her demons.

Melville, Greg

Greasy Rider: Two Dudes, One Fry-Oil-Powered Car, and a Cross-Country Search for a Greener Future. 2008. Algonquin Books of Chapel Hill, ISBN 9781565125957, 257p. 📖.

Melville converted an old diesel Mercedes into a veggiemobile that ran on used cooking grease and headed across the United States with his friend

Iggy to prove it could be done. In this memoir, puns (Melville dubs the trip a "Fuel's Errand") are mixed in with serious thoughts about renewable energy and biofuels. Side trips take Melville to Tennessee to visit Al Gore's home and the National Renewable Energy Laboratory.

Steinbeck, John
Travels with Charley: In Search of America. 2002 (1962). Penguin, ISBN 0142000701, 214p. 📖.

In 1960, toward the end of his writing career, Steinbeck wanted to reacquaint himself with the United States, so he bought a camper truck, and took off with his standardbred poodle Charley on a cross-country jaunt from Sag Harbor, New York, to California, and back again. He stopped in small towns to hear at firsthand what people were thinking and doing and while he loved the changing landscape, he found himself increasingly disillusioned with the materialism and apathy of the people he met. An acute and insightful travelogue that still has relevance after more than 40 years.

Theroux, Paul
The Old Patagonian Express: By Train Through the Americas. 1997 (1979). Houghton Mifflin, ISBN 039552105X, 404p.

Starting out from his Boston home, Theroux traveled south mainly by train, crossing into Mexico and continuing down the entire length of South America until he reached the wild, desert landscape of Patagonia. He records the prejudices and foibles of the people he meets and comments on culture and landscape. Although he can be cranky and impatient at times, he is always a rewarding travel companion. Theroux has written other books about his travels around the world by train, among them *The Great Railway Bazaar, Riding the Iron Rooster,* and *Dark Star Safari.*

Primal Scenes: Vivid Childhood Memoirs

Many of our most vivid memories are from childhood; these remarkably photogenic stories of growing up in various places around the world are particularly good examples. The writers capture other times and places with wonderful fidelity. There's nothing dry about these memoirs; they make history come alive with personal details, vivid descriptions, and interesting characters.

Aciman, Andre

Out of Egypt: A Memoir. 2007 (1994). Picador/Farrar, Straus and Giroux, ISBN 9780312426552, 339p.

Aciman grew up in Alexandria, Egypt, part of a large, close-knit, contentious Jewish clan that settled there in 1905. Fabulous stories of fortunes made and lost, long-running family feuds, sumptuous parties, and summer houses on the beach provide the background to Aciman's nostalgic look at his childhood in the 1950s and 1960s. Even after it was clear that Egypt was unsafe for Jews, Aciman's parents held out until the last moment before leaving their beloved city.

Athill, Diana

Yesterday Morning: A Very English Childhood. 2002. Granta Books, ISBN 978–862075511, 169p.

Athill's upper-class English childhood on her family's estate following World War I was idyllic in many ways. Siblings and cousins rode horses, played in beautiful gardens, and were schooled in the unwritten rules of the English gentry. But there were dark and troubling undercurrents: her parents' unhappy marriage, a father who was mostly absent, and financial problems. A tantalizing, literate portrait of a bygone era, particularly notable for Diana's heartfelt and unsentimental account of her relationship with her mother. Athill's memoirs about her adult life include *Stet: An Editor's Life* and *Somewhere Towards the End: A Memoir.*

Chen, Da

Colors of the Mountain. 2000. Random House, ISBN 0375502882, 310p. 📖.

With the arrival of the Cultural Revolution, Chen's family, formerly landlords, became pariahs in their village, reviled, stripped of their livelihood, and reduced to poverty. Chen was an outcast at school, often humiliated by students and teachers, but he and his parents coped undaunted. Chen's coming-of-age in this setting is a cheering tale of optimism and resilience.

Heller, Joseph

Now and Then: From Coney Island to Here. 1998. Alfred A. Knopf, ISBN 0375400621, 259p.

In this heartfelt and nostalgic memoir, novelist Heller writes about the 1930s and 1940s in the diverse Coney Island neighborhood of Brooklyn that he calls "an ethnic stronghold," where children grew up in the streets and everyone struggled to make ends meet in the thick of the Depression.

Hickam, Homer
Rocket Boys: A Memoir. 1998. Delacorte Press, ISBN 038533320X, 368p. 📖.

When the Russians launched Sputnik, teenaged Homer Hickam, in Coalwood, West Virginia, was inspired to launch his own rockets. To the dismay of his father, the mine superintendent in their company town, Homer and his friends learned the physics of rocket propulsion by trial and error and, in so doing, changed their lives. This is an inspiring memoir about the power of imagination and love. It was turned into the film *October Sky.* Hickam's subsequent memoir, *The Coalwood Way,* covers his senior year in high school.

Jaffrey, Madhur
⇨ *Climbing the Mango Trees: A Memoir of a Childhood in India.* 2006. Alfred A. Knopf, ISBN 9781400042951, 297p.

Food and family are deliciously intertwined in this nostalgic memoir set in and around Delhi in the 1940s and 1950s by the woman whose cookbooks introduced Indian food to Western palates. As part of a large, extended family, tomboy Jaffrey climbed the trees in the family orchard to eat spicy snacks with a gang of siblings and cousins. Her fond memories of banquets, legendary mountain picnics, and Indian street food will have readers hungry to try the recipes she includes. Jaffrey also describes how the turbulence surrounding India's independence and the Partition of Pakistan affected her family.

McCourt, Frank
Angela's Ashes: A Memoir. 1996. Scribner, ISBN 0684874350, 364p. AW. 📖.

Reversing the traditional immigrants' journey, McCourt's impoverished parents moved back to Ireland from New York. His father drank up whatever small wages he earned, leaving his mother barely able to feed and clothe the children, who learned to survive (if they did) in the streets. McCourt's clear-eyed descriptions of the horrors of his early years are riveting.

Smith, Mary-Ann Tirone
Girls of Tender Age: A Memoir. 2007. Free Press, ISBN 9780743279772, 285p.

Smith's Hartford housing project in the 1950s was like a friendly, small town and her large Italian-French family was filled with lovable and eccentric characters. She spent summers at the beach, fished for eels with her grandfather, ate her Uncle Guido's incomparable *bagna cauda,* and coped with her brother's autism. The shadow on the horizon was a child molester who stole away the innocent heart of the neighborhood. This is a nostalgic memoir with a finely honed edge of tension.

Small Is Beautiful: Life in Rural America

For many city and suburb dwellers, the small towns and country places where our families lived are the homes we hold in our hearts, even if we don't want to live there now. These writers paint vivid pictures for us of the pleasures and hardships of rural life, taking us back to times when life was slower and simpler.

Brokaw, Tom

A Long Way from Home: Growing Up in the American Heartland. 2002. Random House, ISBN 0375507639, 233p.

The well-known news anchor and author of *The Greatest Generation* offers reflections about his South Dakota childhood in the 1940s and 1950s. His large, close-knit family valued hard work and the respect that it brought in the community. Church suppers, school sports, and family gatherings filled his days in a world that was light-years away from the political and social changes of that era. His recall of another time and place is gracious and appealing.

Kalish, Mildred Armstrong

Little Heathens: Hard Times and High Spirits on an Iowa Farm During the Great Depression. 2007. Bantam Books, ISBN 9780553804959, 292p. 📖.

"Endure deprivation without complaining; mind your manners at all times; do as your elders say." These were the character-building precepts of Kalish's childhood. This homely and utterly delightful memoir brings to life a lost time and place when life was difficult but the rewards of family and friendship were great. The book is filled with recipes, poems, songs, and satisfying family stories.

Kelton, Elmer

Sandhills Boy: The Winding Trail of a Texas Writer. 2007. Forge Books, ISBN 9780765315212, 252p.

Kelton's heart is in the west Texas cattle country he portrayed in his many novels. His father, a hard-working ranch foreman, expected his son to follow the cowboy life, but Kelton didn't have the talent for it. In this low-key, charming memoir, Kelton offers a gently humorous picture of ranch life in the 1930s, his army service, and how he found his Austrian bride.

Kimmel, Haven

➯ *A Girl Named Zippy: Growing Up Small in Mooreland, Indiana.* 2001. Doubleday, ISBN 0385499825, 275p. 📖.

Kimmel grew up in sleepy Mooreland, Indiana, a town that—mysteriously—always remained at a population of 300. She was nicknamed Zippy as a toddler because of the cute way she ran around, but her parents worried because she didn't speak until she was three. Kimmel's keen eye for the details of small-town life in the 1960s, and a trove of stories about the eccentric doings of her family and community, enliven this tender memoir.

Marquart, Debra

The Horizontal World: Growing Up Wild in the Middle of Nowhere. 2006. Counterpoint, ISBN 9781582433455, 270p.

Marquart's vignettes of growing up as the wild youngest daughter of a sober, hardworking North Dakota farm family capture her burning need to leave a provincial place for the wider world. After years of staying away, she began to feel the need to return and honor her childhood home. Poetic, tender, and funny, she infuses the stark landscape of North Dakota with meaning and metaphor.

Roland, Gwen, with photographs by C. C. Lockwood

Atchafalaya Houseboat: My Years in the Louisiana Swamp. 2006. Louisiana State Univ. Press, ISBN 0807130893, 161p.

In the 1970s, Roland and her partner Calvin Voisin, both in their 20s, lived on a houseboat at Bloody Bayou in the Atchafalaya Swamp, recreating the lifestyle of their ancestors. Roland, a natural storyteller, writes about their easygoing life of fishing and growing their own food. She also tells the stories of their swampland neighbors and of the photographer who brought them fame when his pictures appeared in *National Geographic Magazine*.

Under African Skies

The memoirs on this list were written by people who were fascinated with Africa: the land and the people, the cultures, and the politics. These travelers, pilgrims, writers, and reporters make Africa come alive in all its fascinating diversity.

Dinesen, Isak, (pseudonym of Karen Blixen)
Out of Africa. 1987 (1938). Crown Publishers, ISBN 0517565099, 288p. 📖.

"I had a farm in Africa" is the lovely, understated opening of this classic memoir by Karen Blixen, who came to Kenya in 1913 as a newlywed and chose to stay on after her divorce. Through years of isolation and struggle on the farm, she developed reserves of courage and self- reliance, but her romantic connection with the landscape and the people is what brings this lyrical narrative to life.

Fuller, Alexandra
Don't Let's Go to the Dogs Tonight: An African Childhood. 2001. Random House, ISBN 0375507507, 301p. 📖.

Fuller grew up in Rhodesia, Zambia and Malawi in the 1970s during the time when the British were forced to relinquish their hold on those countries; there was unrest and terrorism wherever they lived. Her family's unusual lifestyle on isolated farms, coupled with her mother's outrageous behavior, is told from a child's wide-eyed point of view with humor and insight. Fuller's love of the African landscape shines through everything she writes.

Godwin, Peter
⇨ *When a Crocodile Eats the Sun: A Memoir of Africa.* 2007. Little, Brown, and Co., ISBN 9780316158947, 344p. 📖. **AW**.

A father's illness and death frame this moving and melancholy story of change and loss. Godwin, a journalist, grew up in Zimbabwe, where his mother was a doctor and his father an engineer. When his father fell ill, Godwin returned to Harare, the first of several trips to visit his aging parents and record the violent collapse of the country. In the process, he uncovered his father's secret history; by the end of the memoir, both family and country are changed forever.

Hofmann, Corinne, trans. by Peter Miller
The White Masai. 2005. Amistad, ISBN 9780061131523, 307p.

On vacation in Kenya, Hoffman spots a Masai warrior, complete with face paint, jewelry, and long red braids. Love hits her like a bolt from the blue and despite the vast cultural differences between them she sells her business in Switzerland and returns to marry Lketinga, live in his remote village in a dung hut, and bear his child. Hofmann tells the provocative story of what happened when she abandoned all for love.

Markham, Beryl

West with the Night. 1983 (1942). North Point Press, ISBN 0865471185, 293p.

Markham came to East Africa as a small child in 1906 with her father, a great horseman. Her lyrical memoir describes her great love of the African landscape and natives and her work with her father as a horse trainer, but it is the sections on her career as a bush pilot in the 1930s that have made this work a well-loved classic.

Shaffer, Tanya

Somebody's Heart Is Burning: A Woman Wanderer in Africa. 2003. Vintage Books, ISBN 1400032598, 324p.

Shaffer's lifelong wanderlust—and fear of commitment to boyfriend Michael—took her to Ghana, Mali, and Kenya for a year when she was 27. She worked as a volunteer, immersing herself in village life and relationships with Africans, Americans, and Europeans with determination and exuberance. Her colorful stories are filled with the complex lessons learned by a white woman open to contact with African culture.

Tayler, Jeffrey

Angry Wind: Through Muslim Black Africa by Truck, Bus, Boat, and Camel. 2005. Houghton Mifflin, ISBN 061833467X, 252p.

Tayler combines engrossing travel writing with incisive journalism in this account of his travels from Chad to Senegal, across the Sahel, the inhospitable desert-like terrain on the southern edge of the Sahara. He survived corrupt border officials, nasty political situations, and fractious vehicles, to depict an explosive tribal world that we ignore at our peril.

Chapter Four

Language

Language is often invisible when we're reading—it's the background, the vehicle, "the raw material out of which literature is crafted," as Francine Prose says in her excellent book *Reading Like a Writer*.[1] But sometimes language takes center stage and we savor the writer's unique voice. Maybe it's humor that catches our attention, elegant imagery, a style that's polished, or one that's conversational. Or maybe the author just knows how to choose the right word to set us laughing, crying, thinking, or nodding in understanding. Language can be the deciding factor in whether we like a book or not. If an author's style doesn't appeal to us, we won't enjoy reading his writing.

Stylistically, these memoirs are diverse and that's what makes them exciting. Anyone who's heard stand-up comedian Paula Poundstone is sure to recognize her voice as they chuckle over *There's Nothing in This Book I Meant to Say*. At the other end of the spectrum, Israeli novelist Amos Oz's memoir of his childhood and adolescence in Jerusalem, *A Tale of Love and Darkness*, is intense, stylistically complex, and totally absorbing. In between, there are lyrical, confiding, homespun, incisive, painful, and exuberant memoirs for every taste.

It can be hard to tell from book reviews what an author's style is like and whether we'll like it. The lists in this chapter can help readers find books in which language is a large part of the appeal. Since language and mood are closely related, it may be helpful to peruse these chapters together.

99

The Definite Article: Writers on Their Lives

In this list, well-known prose masters tell how they learned their craft and how their lives and works are intertwined. Whether you are a fan of their other writing or not, you will enjoy their thoughtful, reflective voices.

Clemens, Samuel Langhorne
Life on the Mississippi by Mark Twain. 2007 (1883). Modern Library ISBN 9780375759376, 364p.

> The teenaged Clemens found steamboat life irresistible; he talked himself into a position as a cub pilot so he could learn to read the great River's ever-changing course. He writes about his years as a pilot from 1857 to 1861; in the second part, he recounts a return trip as a passenger at the end of the steamboats' heyday. Clemens's colorful stories about life on the river are distinguished by the humor and style that remind us why he is still one of our greatest writers.

Hillerman, Tony
Seldom Disappointed: A Memoir. 2001. HarperCollins, ISBN 0060194456, 341p.

> Hillerman, author of a much-loved detective series set in Navajo country, recalls his childhood in small-town Oklahoma, his formative experiences in the army during World War II, and the writing career and marriage that followed. Despite the lack of drama—no child abuse, drugs, or major tragedies—Hillerman's memoir is compelling for its deft portraits of people and places and his homespun, candid prose. Fans of his mysteries are in for a treat.

Hurston, Zora Neale
Dust Tracks on a Road. 1991 (1942). HarperPerennial, ISBN 0060552840, 277p. 📖.

> Anthropologist and novelist Hurston, one of the most famous members of the Harlem Renaissance, was born in 1891 in Eatonville, Florida, an all-black incorporated town that was a nurturing environment for the strong-willed girl. Hurston's very personal and engaging account of her childhood, education, and rise to prominence looks back on all the "sharp shadows, high lights, and smudgy inbetweens."

Lessing, Doris
⇨ *Under My Skin: Volume 1 of My Autobiography, to 1949.* 1994. HarperCollins, ISBN 0060171502, 419p. 📖.

> In this wonderful memoir of intellectual development and growing up at odds with family, Lessing writes about her childhood in rural Southern

Rhodesia (she was born in 1919), and combines vivid descriptions of her internal life with social commentary. She was determined to break free of her parents' expectations and recounts how two failed marriages and involvement with the Communist Party set her on a fiercely independent course. Those who have read Lessing's early novels set in Africa will enjoy this glimpse of the raw materials.

Miller, Arthur

Timebends: A Life. 1995 (1987). Penguin Books ISBN 0140249176, 614p. AW

Miller has penned some of the most enduring plays of the 20th century: *Death of a Salesman, The Crucible, All My Sons.* His own life has been full of drama, and this graceful, insightful memoir reveals the sources of his plays, his relationship with Marilyn Monroe and other well-known figures in the performing arts, and the significant events of his early upbringing in Harlem.

Nabokov, Vladimir

Speak, Memory: An Autobiography Revisited. 1999 (1966). Alfred A. Knopf, ISBN 0375405534, 268p. AW. 📖.

Nabokov's Proustian memoir of his privileged early 20th-century Russian childhood is stunning for the splendor of his recall of that vanished time. "Through a tremulous prism" he brings us lovely, sensual descriptions and reveries about family members, tutors, elegant homes, and vacations, along with insights into how he became a writer. Patient readers will be richly rewarded.

Simon, Neil

Rewrites: A Memoir. 1996. Simon & Schuster, ISBN 0684826720, 397p.

The author of some our most beloved comedies (*The Odd Couple, Come Blow Your Horn, Plaza Suite*) turns to his own life and the sources of his inspiration. With warmth and humor, Simon reveals more than the details of his journey to success, he provides insight into the craft of playwriting and the nurturing relationships with family and friends that helped him thrive.

Talese, Gay

A Writer's Life. 2006. Alfred A. Knopf, ISBN 0679410961, 429p.

Talese's signature style of engaged, incisive journalism fills this dense memoir of people he's known and written about, his childhood on the Jersey Shore, and the details of his writing life. Readers meander with Talese as he explores the subjects that have kept him writing and researching through the years, including sports, celebrity, and sex.

Depth of Field: Insightful Writers

In photography, depth of field refers to the way a lens is used to bring a subject into focus. Similarly, in this group of autobiographical essays, the writers focus in on people, places, and events, bringing out the lights and shadows and burning in their significance. The authors are more interested in extracting meaning from their experiences than in giving us a straight narrative of their lives.

Angell, Roger
Let Me Finish. 2006. Harcourt, ISBN 9780151013500, 302p.

> *The New Yorker* writer Angell, celebrated for his baseball reportage, offers not a chronological autobiography but exquisitely written vignettes that read like the best short fiction. "Peeling back the leaves of memory," he turns a car mishap when he was seven, his childhood love of movies and baseball, or thoughts about his stepfather E. B. White into meditations on how we remember our lives.

Brice, Jennifer
Unlearning to Fly. 2007. University of Nebraska Press, ISBN 9780803210943, 202p.

> Alaska in the 1950s and 1960s was a harsh and beautiful place, where people proudly ignored the news from the lower 48. Brice, daughter of "a Southern stump-logger and an East Coast socialite," experienced the 1964 earthquake, drove a dump truck in the Aleutians, wrote obituaries for the Fairbanks newspaper, and almost learned to take flying small planes in stride. Her stories about flying and what it taught her about herself and others are luminous and enlightening.

Delbridge, Melissa J.
Family Bible. 2008. University of Iowa Press, ISBN 9781587296512, 143p.

> Delbridge's memories of 1960s Tuscaloosa have the sound and smell of the real South in that era. Her father was a charmer whose week-long hunting trips didn't always involve animals; her mother was loving but tough, and left him. Precocious Delbridge ran with a fast crowd, saw the pain, racism, and absurdity in the lives around her and transformed it into fierce and moving prose.

Hansen, Eric

The Bird Man and the Lap Dancer: Close Encounters with Strangers. 2004. Pantheon, ISBN 0375421262, 228p.

You may not have thought that you were interested in the Grand Hotel on Thursday Island or fish smuggling in the Maldives, but Hansen's travel essays will change your mind. He senses that he's "a human magnet" for interesting experiences in out-of-the-way places, and he knows how to mine those experiences for the details that make his stories absorbing. The essay about working at Mother Teresa's clinic in Calcutta, "Life Lessons from Dying Strangers," is especially memorable.

Hogan, Linda

Woman Who Watches Over the World: A Native Memoir. 2001. W.W. Norton & Co., ISBN 0393050181, 207p.

As a Chickasaw Indian, Hogan felt that her tribal identity was her destiny, that "history, like geography, lives in the body." With sorrow, she details how the tragic legacy of American Indian abuse played out in her own life and the lives of her adopted daughters, mixing in myths and stories of Native American wisdom. This is a touching memoir filled with rare, poetic imagery.

Montross, Christine

Body of Work: Meditations on Mortality from the Human Anatomy Lab. 2007. Penguin Press, ISBN 9781594201257, 295p. 📖.

Every medical student survives the first-year human anatomy class, including the complete dissection of a human cadaver, but not everyone could write about the experience with such grace and insight. Montross brings the reader into the room with her, sharing her fears, tears, and growing awareness of the ways in which this difficult experience creates sensitive medical practitioners. While she doesn't emphasize the graphic details, this is not for the squeamish.

O'Faolain, Nuala

Are You Somebody?: The Accidental Memoir of a Dublin Woman. **2nd ed.** 1996. Henry Holt, ISBN 9780805089875, 227p. 📖.

O'Faolain's piercingly honest and beautifully written memoir tells of how she groped her way through a dismal childhood near Dublin in the 1940s and 1950s, a time when "Ireland was a living tomb for women." She writes about her years of searching for love and a meaningful life, her own bouts with alcohol and depression, and her satisfying career as a popular opinion columnist for *The Irish Times.*

Salzman, Mark
⇨ *Iron and Silk.* 1986. Vintage Books, ISBN 0394755111, 211p.

Salzman grew up in suburban Connecticut where he developed a love of China and Chinese martial arts. He studied Chinese in college, and after graduation found a job teaching English at a medical school in Changsha. He writes without pretension or fanfare about his attempts to understand the people he met and the loneliness of always being the outsider. He also writes hilariously of his encounters with a great martial arts teacher. This is a quiet classic, a gem about bridging the gaps between cultures. Salzman wrote about his childhood in the memoir *Lost in Place.*

Full Disclosure: Writing from the Heart

These very literary authors bare their souls for us; we hear their voices in our ears as if we were sharing a cup of coffee at their kitchen tables. They explore good news and bad, friendships, hardships, and difficult emotional states.

Allende, Isabel, trans. by Margaret Sayers Peden
The Sum of Our Days. 2008. Harper, ISBN 9780061551833, 301p.

Novelist Allende's previous memoir, *Paula,* recounted the death of her beloved daughter; here she writes to Paula of the 13 emotion-packed years since that fateful day. Allende is immersed in the lives of family and friends, sharing their many joys and sorrows, opening her home and heart to them in her wish "to live passionately to the very end." Readers of her novels will recognize the sources of her exuberant, magical characters in her own personality and life.

Angelou, Maya
I Know Why the Caged Bird Sings. 2002 (1970). Random House, ISBN 0375507892, 281p. AW. 📖.

In this engaging but often painful memoir, Angelou captures the texture of life for a young African American girl growing up in the 1930s and 1940s. She and her brother lived with relatives in several cities; she brings these places and a varied cast of characters to life with emotional depth and energy. The story of how she found her own voice and struggled against racial prejudice has rarely been so convincingly told. Angelou has written five more autobiographical works, including *Gather Together in My Name* and *All God's Children Need Traveling Shoes.*

Gilbert, Elizabeth

⇨ *Eat, Pray, Love: One Woman's Search for Everything Across Italy, India and Indonesia.* 2006. Viking Press, ISBN 9780670034710, 334p. 📖.

After a painful divorce and a breakup with her lover, Gilbert embarked on a healing journey through three landscapes, Italy, India, and Indonesia, in an effort to connect with God and find inner peace. What she found challenged her view of herself and gave her spiritual nourishment. Her warm, funny, reflective, and very personal voice make her an ideal guide on this unusual and fast-moving journey.

Hampl, Patricia

The Florist's Daughter. 2007. Harcourt, ISBN 9780151012572, 227p. 📖.

At her dying mother's bedside, Hampl thought about how it happened that she remained in St. Paul, Minnesota, living close to her middle-class parents. Her Czech father was a florist who created dazzling designs for upper-crust mansions and charity balls; her mother lived in the realm of language with a storyteller's eye for nuance and the striking detail. Hampl's rich prose examines their "faultlessly ordinary lives" in mid-century America and turns those lives into something quite extraordinary. Hampl wrote an earlier memoir titled *A Romantic Education.*

Monette, Paul

Borrowed Time: An AIDS Memoir. 1988. Harcourt, Brace, Jovanovich, ISBN 0151135983, 342p. 📖.

In this haunting memoir, Monette recalls the desperate time of the early 1980s, when AIDS was "a slowly dawning horror" and every phone call brought bad news. The unthinkable happened when Roger, Monette's beloved partner, was diagnosed with the disease. Angry and devastated, but always eloquent, Monette turns tragedy into an artistic tour de force. His earlier memoir *Becoming a Man: Half a Life Story* is about growing up gay.

Patchett, Ann

Truth and Beauty: A Friendship. 2004. HarperCollins, ISBN 0060572140, 257p. 📖.

Patchett met Lucy Grealy when they were undergraduates but it was at the Iowa Writer's Workshop that their friendship developed a remarkable intensity. Grealy suffered from cancer as a child and lost part of her jaw; she underwent multiple surgeries and suffered from debilitating symptoms, physical and psychological. She and Patchett were lifelines for each other as they struggled to become writers. Patchett's portrait of a uniquely talented and tormented woman is wrenching to read, but riveting in its intensity. Grealy's own account of growing up disfigured is found in *Autobiography of a Face.*

Styron, William

Darkness Visible: A Memoir of Madness. 1990. Random House, ISBN 0394588886, 84p.

In a poignant example of how mental illness is no respecter of success and privilege, critically acclaimed novelist Styron tells how he was overtaken by feelings of worthlessness that escalated into desperate depression. In a frightening turn of events, his sense of loss and dread took him to the brink of suicide. With the stylistic gifts that informed his novels, he helps readers understand the joyless world of depression.

Terkel, Studs, with Sydney Lewis

Touch and Go: A Memoir. 2007. New Press, ISBN 9781595580436, 269p.

Terkel, well known for his oral histories, tells his own entertaining story, filled with incident and character. He grew up in Chicago, where his mother ran a boarding house, came of age in the Depression, served in the Air Force in World War II, and only by chance ended up an oral historian. Rambling and warm, Terkel weaves his own story into the history of the 20th century.

The Great Outdoors:
Communing with Nature

These writers have a strong response to the beauty and variety of the natural world; through their writing we can share their passion.

Abbey, Edward

Desert Solitaire: A Season in the Wilderness. 1990 (1968). Simon & Schuster, ISBN 0671695886, 269p.

Abbey spent three seasons as a park ranger in Arches National Monument in the Utah desert, reveling in the beauty and solitude of his 33,000-acre backyard. In this still-relevant classic of radical environmentalism, he meditates with passion and wit on the future of cowboys, Native Americans, and wilderness, and rails against the effects of "industrial tourism" on the natural landscape.

Beston, Henry

The Outermost House: A Year of Life on the Great Beach of Cape Cod. 1988 (1928). Penguin Books, ISBN 014017012X, 222p.

Naturalist Beston built a house for himself in the 1920s, a little getaway cottage, on the beach near Eastham on Cape Cod. At the end of August, when he should have packed up to go home, he could not tear himself away and decided to stay for a year, to enjoy the changing seasons at the shore. With Beston, we walk the beach in all weathers, watch the birds, and adjust to nature's rhythms. In 1964, his little house was made a National Literary Landmark.

Darwin, Charles
The Voyage of the Beagle. 2004 (1909). National Geographic Society, ISBN 0792265599, 459p.

Darwin's account of his journey from 1831 to 1836 as a naturalist on board a British survey ship is filled with lively, intelligent descriptions of the places, animals, plants, and people he encountered, primarily in South America. He felt lucky to have this opportunity to study the natural world and his enthusiasm never flagged. This is armchair travel at its best, in the company of a great scientific observer.

Dillard, Annie
Pilgrim at Tinker Creek. 1998 (1974). HarperPerennial ISBN 0060953020, 288p. AW

Dillard's nature writing is astonishing: tough and beautiful, filled with vivid images. She lives near Tinker Creek in Virginia and greets each day like an adventurer on a new planet, noticing every change of sky, insect, plant, and animal. Her memoir of one year on Tinker Creek explores "the texture of the world" in her small piece of nature without sentimentality but with remarkable understanding and depth.

Durrell, Gerald
⇨ *My Family and Other Animals.* 2000 (1957). Penguin, ISBN 014028902X, 273p.

In 1933, when Durrell was eight years old, his family moved to the sunny, good-natured Greek island of Corfu. For Durrell it was a kind of paradise; he tramped around with his faithful dog, Roger, investigating the flora and fauna and making friends with the locals. His rapturous descriptions of Corfu and his hilarious stories about his eccentric siblings and long-suffering mother have made this a classic.

Fletcher, Colin
The Man Who Walked Through Time: The Story of the First Trip Afoot Through the Grand Canyon. 1989 (1967). Vintage Books, ISBN 0679723064, 247p.

Fletcher, author of *The Complete Walker,* was an inspiration to hikers and backpackers. He recounts his 400 mile journey on foot through the Grand Canyon, marveling in its timeless beauty and the restorative powers of its solitude. A classic memoir with insightful nature writing and practical advice to the adventurous walker.

Keenan, Brian

Four Quarters of Light: An Alaskan Journey. 2006. Broadway Books, ISBN 9780767923255, 364p. 📖.

    Jack London's *Call of the Wild* made a strong impression on Keenan as a child; he always felt drawn to wild, desolate places for their transformational qualities. After a brief trip to Fairbanks, he returned to Alaska for an extended stay, intoxicated by the magnificent vistas and unusual people. Open to every experience, he lived with an Inuit shaman, learned how to drive a dogsled, camped in the tundra, skinned hides, and reveled in the life-altering wildness of the landscape.

Ray, Janisse

Ecology of a Cracker Childhood. 1999. Milkweed Editions, ISBN 157131234X, 285p.

    Ray grew up in rural southern Georgia, in a house set in the middle of a junkyard, with parents who scrimped and bartered. She vividly recounts the dramas in her family history: stories of childhood escapades, her wild grandfather Charlie, her father's bout with mental illness. Ray's connection to the landscape is strong and emotional; chapters about vanishing forests and wildlife are witness to the abuses of civilization.

Loud and Clear: Unique Voices

    Watch out for the unique personalities here—their provocative voices make their stories hard to forget. They are written in very different styles, as befits the authors' distinctive personalities; each one is haunting in its own way.

Facey, A. B.

⇨ *A Fortunate Life.* 1984. Viking Press, ISBN 0670803073, 342p. 📖.

    Born in 1894, Facey was an orphan by age two, raised by his grandmother until he was eight when he was hired out as an itinerant farm worker. He survived the battle of Gallipoli in World War I, only to face financial and physical setbacks, and the loss of his son in the following years. Despite a life of unthinkable hardship, he considered himself fortunate, accepting and rejoicing in life. This riveting memoir is a classic in Australia for the author's unflinching, courageous, beautifully told life story, which encapsulates much of Australia's modern history.

Greene, Gael

Insatiable: Tales from a Life of Delicious Excess. 2006. Warner Books, ISBN 9780446576994, 368p.

The title refers to food and sex: both appetites take center stage in this knowing tell-all. Former *New York Magazine* food critic Greene shares her life of sensuous excess, starting with a tryst with Elvis in 1956. Greene has eaten at all the great restaurants, partied with famous names in the food world, and enjoyed affairs with well-known actors, chefs, and others.

Holland, Endesha Ida Mae

From the Mississippi Delta: A Memoir. 1997. Simon & Schuster, ISBN 0684810115, 318p. 📖.

Raped on her 11th birthday by her white employer, Holland started on a path of prostitution and petty crime. She was desperate for an escape route from the grinding poverty and repression she saw around her; when civil rights workers came to her home town, she signed on as an organizer. Her long road from there to a Ph.D. is filled with tragedies and successes, all told in her unique Delta voice.

Marchetto, Marisa Acocella

Cancer Vixen: A True Story. 2006. Alfred A. Knopf, ISBN 9780307263575, 211p.

Three weeks before her wedding to sexy New York restaurateur Silvano, cartoonist Marchetto was diagnosed with breast cancer. As a high maintenance fashionista with a fast-paced New York life, she had no room in her date book for a life-threatening medical problem. Marchetto has created a funny, stylish, and very poignant graphic narrative to show and tell how she coped with medical decisions and treatments and picked up some important life lessons along the way.

Poundstone, Paula

There's Nothing in This Book That I Meant to Say. 2006. Harmony Books, ISBN 9780609603161, 274p.

Only stand-up comedian Poundstone could riff off the lives of Joan of Arc, Helen Keller, and Abraham Lincoln in a way that respects their greatness while making us laugh about her own life. Her three adopted children, their pets—including the dog she's sure is part shark—are all grist for her trademark stream-of-consciousness humor. She doesn't shy away from writing about the alcohol abuse that brought her a DWI and child molestation conviction.

Singer, Isaac Bashevis

In My Father's Court. 1966. Farrar, Straus and Giroux, ISBN 9780374505929, 307p. AW. 📖.

Singer's father was a rabbi in Warsaw who ruled on matters of Jewish law. The cases were of many kinds, often touching on issues of deep, personal significance. Singer loved to eavesdrop on these sessions as a young boy, soaking up scholarly wisdom and psychological insight and reveling in the personal details. A master storyteller, Singer's recreation of his childhood in this vanished Yiddish world of the early 20th century is unique and engaging. Singer also published *More Stories from My Father's Court.*

Spiegelman, Art

Maus: A Survivor's Tale; I: My Father Bleeds History. 1986. Pantheon, ISBN 0394747232, 159p. 📖.

Spiegelman, comic book artist and son of Holocaust survivors, records his father Vladek's Holocaust story in graphic form. In the present, Spiegelman navigates a trying relationship with his father in the shadow of Vladek's horrific past. The visual representation of Vladek's plight, with Jews depicted as mice and Nazis as cats adds a unique intensity. Part II, *And Here My Troubles Began,* follows Vladek into the camps. This was one of the first memoirs written in graphic form and still one of the most remarkable.

Luminous Prose: Elegant Memoirs

In these life stories the writing may slow down our reading: we want to savor lush descriptive passages and beautiful turns of phrase, maybe even underline our favorite parts, or leave comments in the margins.

Abu-Jaber, Diana

The Language of Baklava: A Memoir. 2005. Pantheon, ISBN 0375423044, 330p.

With an unflappable American mother and an impetuous Jordanian father, Abu-Jaber was never sure how to behave. As a child of two cultures, she observed both with a writer's sensitive eye and regales us with luscious memories of food and family, whether it's under a Bedouin tent in Jordan or at a cookout on the shores of Lake Ontario. She includes recipes that relate to the stories she tells. Readers may also enjoy her novel *Crescent,* about a woman of Iraqi descent.

Danticat, Edwidge
Brother, I'm Dying. 2007. Alfred A. Knopf, ISBN 9781400041152, 272p. AW. 📖.

Danticat's parents left Haiti to find work in New York while she and her brother stayed behind in the care of their uncle Joseph and his wife, leaving her forever committed to two sets of parents and two countries. Years later she recalls the relationships between the two parts of her family and the heart-breaking way that volatile Haitian politics affected their lives. This is a moving memoir of family connections and loss. Readers may also enjoy Danticat's novel *Breath, Eyes, Memory,* about a young girl growing up in Haiti.

Dillard, Annie
⇨ *An American Childhood.* 1987. Harper & Row, ISBN 0060158050, 285p.

Dillard's gift is in her ability to remember and describe in rich three-dimensional prose what she saw and felt growing up in Pittsburgh in the 1950s. An intensely curious child, she examined everything around her, from the skin on her mother's hand to her own developing consciousness of the natural world. Reading her words helps us recall our own childhoods with greater clarity. Dillard is the author of the classic of nature writing, *Pilgrim at Tinker Creek.*

Kingston, Maxine Hong
The Woman Warrior: Memoir of a Girlhood Among Ghosts. 1989 (1976). Vintage International, ISBN 0679721886, 209p. AW. 📖.

Kingston's classic feminist account of the Chinese immigrant experience is unconventional in style, mixing dreamlike recollections of Chinese myths and legends with realistic accounts of first generation Chinese in the United States and her own experiences growing up in San Francisco. The magical realism and shifting points of view enhance our understanding of the dislocating immigrant experience. Kingston followed with a second memoir, about her father, *China Men.*

Marquez, Gabriel Garcia, trans. by Edith Grossman
Living to Tell the Tale: A Memoir. 2003. Alfred A. Knopf, ISBN 1400041341, 483p. 📖.

Readers will find the roots of Marquez's fantastical stories in this enchanting autobiography, which begins when he is in his early twenties and ends five years later, when he proposes to his wife. He recalls his childhood in Colombia, his many eccentric friends and family members, the landscape that inspired his novels and stories, and the moment when he knew he would become a writer.

McCracken, Elizabeth

An Exact Replica of a Figment of My Imagination: A Memoir. 2008. Little, Brown and Co., ISBN 9780316027670, 184p.

Novelist McCracken and her husband Edward were living in France when she became pregnant with the baby they lovingly called "Pudding." Certain they could find adequate health care in their rural area, they waited to become a happy threesome. When the baby was stillborn, their sadness was overwhelming. McCracken's eloquent, moving, and often funny account of their lives in this time is a testament to her grace as a writer.

Orr, Gregory

The Blessing: A Memoir. 2002. Council Oak Books, ISBN 1571781110, 209p. 📖.

When Orr was 12, he accidentally killed his younger brother in a hunting accident, scarring his family and changing his own life forever. In this wise and touching memoir, he reveals how he went on, carrying a terrible burden of guilt and shame, living through hard times as a civil rights worker, and becoming a poet.

Oz, Amos, trans. by Nicholas de Lange

A Tale of Love and Darkness. 2004. Harcourt, ISBN 0151008787, 538p. 📖.

Oz's writes of his childhood in Jerusalem in the 1930s and 1940s with exquisite nuance and recall. He was the precocious only child of an intellectual, self-absorbed father and a beautiful, romantic mother. Through wonderful set pieces we observe Oz's intellectual development and his growing awareness of the adult world, set against the background of Zionist politics. The memoir culminates with his mother's suicide, which changed the trajectory of his life.

Private Worlds: Diaries

People keep diaries for many reasons: to bear witness, for comfort, to note extraordinary events or times, to explore their thoughts in depth, or to leave a legacy. All these reasons and more will be found in the remarkable diaries in this group. Although many diaries are written with an eye to eventual publication, it's still a very personal form, where language reflects the author's immersion in the moment.

Anonymous, trans. by Philip Boehm
➪ *A Woman in Berlin: Eight Weeks in the Conquered City: A Diary.* 2005 (1954). Metropolitan Books/Henry Holt, ISBN 9780805075403, 261p. AW.

When the Soviet Army entered Berlin in April, 1945, the author, a journalist and editor living alone, began this remarkable diary. She and her neighbors were trapped in a nightmarish world with little food and fuel; the occupying soldiers raped, murdered, and looted with impunity. With an unfaltering eye for the telling detail she left this testament to the resilience of the human spirit.

Codell, Esme Raji
Educating Esme: Diary of a Teacher's First Year. 2001. Algonquin Books of Chapel Hill, ISBN 1565122259, 204p. 📖.

Codell's diary takes us into the bullet-scarred fifth grade classroom of a mainly black inner city Chicago school. With guts, creativity, and wisdom beyond her 24 years, she made her classroom a safe place for students, nurturing their academic and social development, despite her principal's disapproval and the heartbreaking home lives of some of her pupils. An updated version was published in 2009.

Filipovic, Zlata
Zlata's Diary: A Child's Life in Wartime Sarajevo, rev. ed. 2006 (1994). Penguin Books, ISBN 0143036874, 197p.

When Filipovic began her diary in the fall of 1991, she was a lighthearted 11-year-old schoolgirl. By spring, she was writing about the daily shelling of the city from the hillside above her home; she and her parents lived in the one safe room in their apartment or huddled in the basement with only intermittent electricity, water, or gas. From a child's viewpoint, but with a mature writer's insight and keen observation, she recorded the war's toll and its pointlessness.

Frank, Anne, trans. by Susan Massotty
The Diary of a Young Girl: The Definitive Edition. 1995 (1952). Doubleday, ISBN 0385473788, 340p. AW. 📖.

In 1940, when the Germans occupied the Netherlands, Frank, a Jewish teenager, went into hiding with her family. They lived for two years in an attic behind a false wall until they were betrayed and sent to Nazi death camps. Frank's diary survived; in it she wrote about how they lived from day to day, but most remarkable is the vibrant voice of a young girl in that terrible time exploring her thoughts and emotions with the insight of an accomplished writer. The diary has become an iconic account of the Holocaust. Readers may be interested in Francine Prose's book about the diary, *Anne Frank: The Book, The Life, The Afterlife,* in which she considers Frank's artistry and the diary's impact.

Klemperer, Victor, trans. by Martin Chalmers
  I Will Bear Witness: A Diary of the Nazi Years, 1933–1941. 1998. Random House, ISBN 0679456961, 519p. AW
    Klemperer's remarkable diaries cover all 12 years of the Third Reich. He and his wife lived in Dresden during this period, witnesses to the progressive humiliation and deportation of the Jewish population; Klemperer, a Jew, was spared because his wife was Protestant. Written in secret, the diaries' candor and directness are absorbing and enlightening. The second volume of the diaries covers the years 1942–1945.

Norris, Kathleen
  The Cloister Walk. 1996. Riverhead Books, ISBN 1573220280, 384p. 📖.
    Norris was raised Protestant and rarely attended church, but she spent extended periods of time at a Benedictine monastery in Minnesota, captivated by the way it refreshed her soul. The liturgical year frames her moving memoir; she meditates on the readings, holidays, the Benedictine Rule, and how the liturgy inspired her return to writing poetry. In a later memoir, *Acedia and Me: Marriage, Monks, and a Writer's Life,* she writes about her struggle with soul-weariness and indifference.

Palin, Michael
  Diaries, 1969–1979: The Python Years. 2007. Thomas Dunne Books/St. Martin's Press, ISBN 9780312369354, 650p.
    This is a must read for Monty Python fans: Palin's diary covers the years when the group was starting up and finding its comic identity. Those who have read Palin's travel memoirs will find the same amiable companion here, with the added bonus of insight into Monty Python's working style and Palin's personal life.

Short and Sweet: Under 200 Pages

When you don't have time to settle in for a long read, try these memoirs that are all less than 200 pages. They have an impact that transcends their length, reminding us of the importance of the well-chosen word.

Allison, Dorothy
Two or Three Things I Know For Sure. 1995. Dutton, ISBN 0525939210, 94p. 📖.

What Allison knows was hard won: how dangerous it is to be beautiful, the legacy of violence in Southern families, and the need to honor our differences. Her bestselling autobiographical novel, *Bastard Out of Carolina,* preceded this memoir; here she writes about the women of her family and of how transforming the physical and emotional burdens of her abused childhood into writing saved her soul.

Beckerman, Ilene
Love, Loss, and What I Wore. 1995. Algonquin Books of Chapel Hill, ISBN 1565121112, 139p. 📖.

With tender drawings of the clothing she wore at crucial times in her life, Beckerman opens a window into the recent past that allows us to recall with her the attitudes and cultural upheavals of the 1950s, 1960s, and 1970s. The stories she tells alongside the Brownie uniforms, strapless dresses, and chemises reveal the heartbreak and happiness of a life fully lived. A quick read with a lasting impression.

Crystal, Billy
⇨ *700 Sundays.* 2005. Warner Books, ISBN 9780446578677, 182p.

Crystal grew up the youngest of three boys in a happy Long Island home where his hard-working father only had Sundays to share with his sons. Through Commodore Records, the jazz label created by his father and uncle, Crystal knew all the jazz greats of the 1960s and was surrounded by people who encouraged his talent. Crystal's memoir is based on his popular one-man Broadway show and delivers the same comic punch and heartfelt tribute to his father.

Cunningham, Laura
Sleeping Arrangements. 1989. Alfred A. Knopf, ISBN 0394561120, 195p.

Cunningham's single mother died when she was eight and her two eccentric bachelor uncles moved into her Bronx apartment to care for her. In this unusual household, food and hygiene weren't high on the agenda, but Len and Gabe did their best to nurture and understand the precocious child they had taken on. This is an offbeat and poignant coming-of-age memoir by a skillful writer.

Gallagher, Dorothy

How I Came Into My Inheritance: And Other True Stories. 2001. Random House, ISBN 0375503463, 187p.

Gallagher's eccentric and cantankerous family members come alive in these hilarious and loving vignettes of life in New York City in the 1940s and 1950s. Her extended family of Communist sympathizers battled with the world and each other. Gallagher published a second collection of autobiographical essays titled *Strangers in the House: Life Stories.*

Kidder, Tracy

My Detachment: A Memoir. 2005. Random House, ISBN 0375506152, 192p.

Kidder joined ROTC in college in the early 1960s without much thought; by the time he graduated and entered the army, the Vietnam War was in full swing and his heart was with the protesters. He was sent to Vietnam and put in charge of eight irritable soldiers to report on enemy radio locations. In this relatively safe posting, Kidder struggled with feelings of melancholy and a sense of inadequacy. No glory of battle here, just a very candid and thoughtful portrayal of a young man and his demons in turbulent times.

Note

1. Francince Prose. *Reading Like a Writer: A Guide for People Who Love Books and for Those Who Want to Write Them.* New York: HarperCollins, 1996, p. 16.

Chapter Five

Mood

What are you in the mood to read? Mood and atmosphere refer to the emotions we feel when we read a book. The writer uses language to evoke a mood in the reader. This may be the most important factor in the way we choose books. If the mood of a book isn't right, we're likely to put it down with a feeling of dissatisfaction. These life stories are distinctive for the way the author has employed language, pacing, description, and other stylistic tools to create a unique atmosphere.

Sometimes we enjoy a book because of its mood, but we don't know how to describe that special something that makes it appealing to us. The lists in this chapter should help readers identify books where the mood is distinctive, for example, nostalgic, humorous, reflective, bleak, inspirational, or edgy. Many of these memoirs introduce us to memorable characters, but their overwhelming appeal is in the atmosphere the author is able to create.

A Backward Glance: Nostalgic Memoirs

Although we can't turn back the clock, we all have times and places that are especially vivid in our memories. In this list, we meet authors who recreate those special times in their lives for us.

Baker, Russell

Growing Up. 1983. New American Library, ISBN 0452255503, 278p. <mark>AW</mark>.

Baker's popular "Observer" column ran in *The New York Times* for many years and was treasured for its gently satirical and self-deprecatory humor. With the same grace and humor, he writes about his early years in rural Virginia and Baltimore during the Depression, his father's early death, and his mother's struggle to raise three children. *Growing Up* won the Pulitzer Prize and was followed by a sequel, *The Good Time.*

Bryson, Bill

⇨ *The Life and Times of the Thunderbolt Kid: A Memoir.* 2006. Broadway Books, ISBN 076791936X, 270p.

Bryson mixes his own story of growing up in Des Moines, Iowa, in the 1950s with social history of that era. He describes his all-American childhood with his distinctive laugh-out-loud humor and wit. The book is filled with dead-on descriptions of 1950s pastimes, pranks, family life, and vacations, all from the point of view of a small Midwestern boy trying very hard to grow up and make sense out of the mysterious adult world around him. For anyone who remembers the 1950s, this is a gem of a memoir.

Edgerton, Clyde

Solo: My Adventures in the Air. 2005. Algonquin Books of Chapel Hill, ISBN 156512426X, 276p.

Edgerton saw his first plane at age four and knew he'd be a pilot. He signed up for Air Force ROTC in college and served in Vietnam as a combat pilot. His enthusiasm for flying never flagged, but his feelings about the Vietnam War turned sour. His memoir is filled with fascinating details of flight mechanics and fighter pilot training, making it a treat for all vicarious pilots and lovers of flight.

Goodison, Lorna

From Harvey River: A Memoir of My Mother and Her Island. 2007. Amistad, ISBN 9780061337550, 288p.

The island is Jamaica, where Goodison's mother was one of the fabulous Harvey sisters, who lived charmed lives in the town named after their paternal grandfather in the early to mid-20th century. Goodison's tale of the rich, interracial mix of island relationships, spiced with patois and poetry, is absorbing and magical.

Goodwin, Doris Kearns
Wait Till Next Year: A Memoir. 1997. Simon & Schuster, ISBN 0684824892, 261p. 📖.

Growing up on Long Island in the 1950s, Goodwin's block was the center of her life: everyone knew everyone else and all the children played together in the streets. Baseball was avidly watched and hotly debated; Goodwin and her father shared a special bond over their love of the sport. Infused with nostalgia, this is a lovely portrait of a young Catholic girl growing to adulthood.

McMurtry, Larry
Books: A Memoir. 2008. Simon & Schuster, ISBN 9781416583349, 259p.

McMurtry is well-known as a bestselling author; here he writes about his lifelong love affair with books, his career as an antiquarian bookseller in Washington, D.C., and his home town of Archer, Texas. He writes about dealers and scouts, the rare books that got away, his personal collection of 28,000 books, his writing life, and his favorite authors in a graceful, rambling style.

O'Neill, Molly
Mostly True: A Memoir of Family, Food, and Baseball. 2006. Scribner, ISBN 9780743232685, 288p.

The subtitle tells it all in this warm-hearted account of growing up the oldest of six (her siblings were all boys) in Columbus, Ohio. Her mother, fanatic housekeeper and cook, was unnerved by the chaos and messes; her father hoped for professional baseball careers and pacified the neighbors. O'Neill recalls her own role as assistant mother and tells how she found her way out of Columbus to a career in food writing.

Valentini, Mario, and Cheryl Hardacre
Chewing Gum in Holy Water: A Childhood in the Heart of Italy. 2006. Arcade Publishing, ISBN 9781559708371, 319p.

With a gently nostalgic tone, Valentini recounts episodes from his childhood, when he lived with his uncle, a traveling priest, in 1950s rural Italy. A curious child, he loved the freedom of moving from town to town and found opportunities for mischief and adventure, all of which we see from a child's perspective. He meets a wolf at dusk, takes on a bull to win the affection of a girl, and learns something about the vulnerabilities of nuns.

Growing Up Absurd: Unusual Childhoods

Family life in these memoirs was, to say the least, unusual, but the authors survived successfully to share their stories with us. There's lots of attitude, eccentricity, and black humor here, as well as insights gained from painful experience.

Bechdel, Alison

⇨ *Fun Home: A Family Tragicomic.* 2006. Houghton Mifflin, ISBN 9780618477944, 232p. AW. 📖.

Bechdel's family ran—and lived in—the local funeral home in a small Pennsylvania town, a Victorian mansion obsessively restored by her father, whose inability to express emotion marked her childhood like a curse. In a remarkable marriage of text and pictures, the funny and tragic aspects of life in the "fun home" are revealed with heartbreaking clarity. As she grows up, Alison comes to understand how her father differs from other fathers, and how she is different as well.

Burroughs, Augusten

Running with Scissors: A Memoir. 2002. St. Martin's Press, ISBN 0312283709, 304p. 📖.

Burroughs' memoir may well take the cake for weirdness and squalor. At the age of 12, his mother left him with her psychiatrist while she worked out her sexual issues. The doctor's household and family were bizarre, complete with a pedophile living in a shed out back and an old electroshock machine in the hall closet. Burroughs portrays all this with a comic detachment and lack of sentimentality that is entertaining in the extreme. He wrote a second memoir, *Dry,* and a memoir about his father, *A Wolf at the Table.*

Gildiner, Catherine

Too Close to the Falls. 2001. Viking Press, ISBN 0312283709, 354p.

Gildiner grew up in a small town near Niagara Falls where her father owned the drugstore. She spent her hyperactive childhood years working long hours there, stocking products and accompanying the deliveryman, Roy, who became her close friend and confidante. Her family never ate at home, hid from visitors, and allowed their unusual child free rein. Hilarious and touching, Gildiner does a great job of portraying her inner life as a child.

Moehringer, J. R.
The Tender Bar: A Memoir. 2005. Hyperion, ISBN 1401300642, 370p. 📖.

Moehringer spent his childhood searching for someone to replace the father who abandoned him and his mother. He found plenty of father figures at Dickens, a feel-good bar in Manhasset, Long Island, where he was befriended by the eccentric regulars. His attachment to the bar and its alcoholic haze was a blessing and a curse. Simultaneously touching and zany, this is an unusual coming-of-age tale.

Narayan, Kirin
My Family and Other Saints. 2007. Univ. of Chicago Press, ISBN 9780226568201, 236p.

Narayan grew up near Bombay with an American mother and an Indian father. In the late 1960s, her older brother Rahoul discovered the hippie, marijuana-smoking wanderers flocking to the area; he left home on a spiritual search to find his own guru, encouraged by his mother while his father retreated into alcohol. As Narayan grew up, her increasingly fractured family members followed Rahoul in their own ways, as she relates in this funny, tender memoir of those unusual times.

Rothschild, Matt
Dumbfounded: A Memoir. 2008. Crown Publishers, ISBN 9780307405425, 301p.

Money was no object in Rothschild's family, but love was in short supply. His jet-setting mother couldn't be bothered to raise him and left him with his wildly mismatched, eccentric grandparents. Their casual approach to child-rearing left Rothschild troubled and lonely: he tells a tragicomic story of acting out at school, running away, and verifying his sexual identity with prostitutes in Times Square. Almost unbelievable but very entertaining, Rothschild mines the dysfunctional family genre for laughs.

Traig, Jennifer
Devil in the Details: Scenes from an Obsessive Girlhood. 2006. Little, Brown and Co., ISBN 0316158771, 246p.

"What teenager spends her free time reading psalms and sterilizing tongs?" asks Traig, whose obsessive compulsive disorder was combined with scrupulosity, a form of hyper-religious fervor brought on by learning about Jewish ritual when she was 12. Traig looks back with candor and zingy one-liners at how she and her family survived her freaky teenage years.

Walls, Jeannette
  The Glass Castle: A Memoir. 2005. Scribner, ISBN 0743247531, 288p. AW. 📕.
    Walls's *The Glass Castle* opens with a description of riding in a taxi in
  Manhattan and spotting her mother rooting in a Dumpster; this scene sets the
  stage for the story of her desperate, vagabond childhood. Her father's talents
  were sabotaged by his paranoia and alcoholism; her mother was an artist who
  thought children should roam free. There was rarely food to eat and they often
  moved in the middle of the night, one step ahead of disaster, abandoning their
  possessions. Amazingly, Walls avoids self-pity and blame to pen a tribute to
  her family's resilience.

Laugh Lines: Memoirs on the Lighter Side

Humor comes in many different styles, as these memoirs demonstrate: zany,
offbeat, exuberant, understated, ironic, or black. For some authors, it's cathartic;
for others, a way to transform their anxieties and frustrations; and some just see
humor in the human condition.

Alexander, William
  ***The $64 Tomato: How One Man Nearly Lost His Sanity, Spent a Fortune, and
  Endured an Existential Crisis in the Quest for the Perfect Garden.*** 2007.
  Algonquin Books of Chapel Hill, ISBN 9781565125032, 304p.
    Mother Nature is a relentless taskmaster, as Alexander finds out when he
  creates a large vegetable garden and orchard behind his New York Hudson
  Valley home, naively anticipating the joys of cultivating the soil. In this hilarious tale, he battles weeds, insects, pesky animals, and contractors; endures the
  scorn of his children and the laughter of his neighbors; and passes on to the
  reader his hard-won practical and philosophical gardening advice.

Bryson, Bill
  A Walk in the Woods: Rediscovering America on the Appalachian Trail. 1998.
  Broadway Books, ISBN 0767902513, 276p.
    After "years of waddlesome sloth," Bryson sets out to hike the Appala-
  chian Trail, which stretches some 2,100 miles from Georgia to Maine. He is
  joined by Katz, a similarly unfit 40-something; they set off from the southern
  end, gamely toting their packs. With his trademark sly and deadpan humor,
  Bryson entertains us with the adventures and trials of the hike and provides
  information about the trail and the landscape.

Cohen, Amy

The Late Bloomer's Revolution: A Memoir. 2007. Hyperion, ISBN 9781401300029, 288p.

It's embarrassing to 30-something Cohen that her latest live-in boyfriend dumped her, she's been fired from her job, her face is disfigured by a nasty rash, and she still can't ride a bicycle. This one-time dating columnist for *The New York Observer* recounts her misadventures on the Manhattan dating scene with a hilarity born of frustration and a sharp eye for the foibles of family, friends, and eligible guys.

Diller, Phyllis, with Richard Buskin

Like a Lampshade in a Whorehouse: My Life in Comedy. 2005. Jeremy P. Tarcher/ Penguin, ISBN 1585423963, 266p.

The queen of self-deprecating humor and wild hair reveals the life story that fueled her act. Diller was born to elderly parents, married Sherwood Diller at an early age, and had six children despite Sherwood's chronic unemployment and mental illness. She broke into the comedy scene in the 1950s, working hard for acceptance as a woman comedian. Reading her life story, it becomes clear how the humor came at the expense of pain.

Hiaasen, Carl

Downhill Lie: A Hacker's Return to a Ruinous Sport. 2008. Alfred A. Knopf, ISBN 9780307266538, 207p.

Novelist Hiaasen, a self-described recidivist golfer, hadn't played in over 30 years. With the same satirical gifts that animate his novels, he skewers his attempts to hit a ball straight down the fairway and break 90. We learn about the new shapes of golf clubs (a club head "the size of Ozzy Osbourne's liver"). He tries wearing a triangular pendant guaranteed to improve his game, tries a "rescue club," and blames his golfing friends for egging him on in a hopeless cause. Hilarious stuff even for non-golfers.

James, Clive

⇨ *Unreliable Memoirs.* 2009 (1981). W.W. Norton & Co., ISBN 9780393336085, 171p.

James pens a hilarious account of growing up in Sydney, Australia, in the 1940s and 1950s, son of a widowed mother who despaired of ever seeing her son make something of himself. His childhood was filled with mischief and over-the-top exploits at school and in the neighborhood, all of which hid his frantic adolescent need for acceptance and sexual conquest. A laugh-out-loud coming-of-age story with a strong sense of place and time.

Leleux, Robert

The Memoirs of a Beautiful Boy. 2008. St. Martin's Press, ISBN 9780312361686, 272p.

Hilarious spot-on descriptions and memorable one-liners mask the pain and confusion of growing up gay on a ranch in Petunia, Texas. Leleux was best friends with his glamour-girl mother and a mystery to his veterinarian father, who left them for his pregnant mistress. Mother turned to desperate plastic surgeries while Leleux fell in love.

Sedaris, David

Dress Your Family in Corduroy and Denim. 2004. Little, Brown and Co., ISBN 0316143464, 257p.

In these personal essays, Sedaris shares childhood memories, digging under the surface to expose humor, angst, and sadness. His mismatched parents, contemplating purchasing a vacation cottage, brightened with "the rejuvenating power of real estate." After too many snow days, his mother locked the children out of the house so she could return to solitary drinking. The mirror that Sedaris holds up to family relationships may be cracked but it's wholly enjoyable.

Wolk, Josh

Cabin Pressure: One Man's Desperate Attempt to Recapture His Youth as a Camp Counselor. 2007. Hyperion, ISBN 1401302602, 273p.

With marriage coming up in September, 34-year-old Wolk can't resist one last visit to Camp Eastwind in Maine, scene of many happy summers. As a counselor to a group of 14-year-old boys, he hears the same hilariously bad jokes, breathes in the same moldy bunk smells, and experiences the same insecurities he felt as a kid. This is a funny and nostalgic tribute to the land of summer camp.

Renewal: Life-Altering Experiences

These authors write about life-altering experiences; their memoirs tantalize us with the possibility of change in our own lives. Some were desperate to shake up their lives; for others, change came unexpectedly.

Albert, John

Wrecking Crew: The Really Bad News Griffith Park Pirates. 2005. Scribner, ISBN 9780743246323, 277p.

Albert and his friends—a raddled group of musicians, screenwriters, and actors on the fringes of Hollywood and in the thick of drugs and alcohol—formed a baseball team to play in a weekly league. Although this is far from a feel-good tale of instant salvation, the group coheres and some find healing in the camaraderie and routine of practice. Funky, hip, and very LA.

Bounds, Gwendolyn
Little Chapel on the River: A Pub, a Town and the Search for What Matters Most. 2005. Wm. Morrow, ISBN 0060564067, 287p.

In September, 2001, Wall Street reporter Bounds and her partner were displaced from their apartment near the World Trade Center. In search of temporary housing they came to Garrison, New York, and Bounds discovered Guinan's bar, a local institution with legendary, eccentric denizens and a charismatic owner. The bar quickly became a focus of her life, providing the sense of community she sorely needed, a connection with her past, and the strength to change her future.

Fergus, Charles
Summer at Little Lava: A Season at the Edge of the World. 1998. North Point Press, ISBN 0374525528, 289p.

Fergus and his wife planned to spend the summer with their young son in a tiny, isolated house near the sea in Iceland; when Fergus's mother was brutally stabbed to death, it seemed even more important to get away. The house, Little Lava, became a refuge and a place to heal, to revel in the stark natural beauty of the mountains and marshes, and study the bird life. Their months enjoying the long hours of summer sun in this hospitable country worked their magic on Fergus's grief.

Fraser, Laura
An Italian Affair. 2001. Pantheon, ISBN 0375420657, 226p. 📖.

Fraser was reeling after her divorce, not sure how to recover her equilibrium. She traveled to Italy to visit friends and practice her Italian; on the island of Ischia she met an older, married French art professor, and they began an affair, meeting periodically in exotic places. In this memoir that combines travel and romance, she tells how the affair healed her heart.

Goldhammer, Catherine
⇨ *Still Life With Chickens: Starting Over in a House by the Sea.* 2006. Hudson Street Press, ISBN 1594630259, 178p. 📖.

After her divorce, Goldhammer couldn't afford the big house in the upscale but heartless community where she never fit in anyway. She found a fixer-upper in a nearby working-class town, and to appease her 12-year-old daughter, agreed to buy six baby chicks. The chicks become the symbol and touchstone for her enchanting tale of transformation and renewal. Goldhammer's second memoir about her life with her daughter is *Winging It: Dispatches from an (Almost) Empty Nest.*

Jourdan, Carolyn

Heart in the Right Place. 2007. Algonquin Books of Chapel Hill, ISBN 9781565124875, 297p. 📖.

At 40, Carolyn Jourdan thought she had it all: life as a high-powered lawyer in Washington, D.C., where her work influenced national energy policies. When her mother had a heart attack, she promised to fill in for her as receptionist in her father's small-town east Tennessee family medical practice for just a few days. This new role in her home town made her think about how we find meaning in our lives and the value of the work we do, and led her to a new understanding of how she wanted to live.

Matthiessen, Peter

The Snow Leopard. 2008 (1978). Penguin Books, ISBN 9780143105510, 336p. AW

In 1973, Matthiessen accompanied naturalist George Schaller to Nepal to search for the rare snow leopard. They trekked for 35 days through wild, snow-covered mountain passes, enduring harsh conditions and visiting the local Nepalese. In this classic account, beloved by fans of nature writing and spirituality, Matthiessen's journey through this wild, mystical landscape becomes a metaphor for understanding personal issues of faith and grief.

Richards, Susan

Chosen by a Horse: A Memoir. 2006. Soho Press, ISBN 9781569474198, 248p. 📖.

Richards was living a solitary life on her New York farm, taking care of three horses and doing her best to recover from abuse, alcohol, and a disastrous marriage when she volunteered to take in a sick mare and foal. The mare, Lay Me Down, with her unexpectedly loving and trusting nature, helped Richards learn some important lessons about life and love among humans in this absorbing and poignant story.

Shulman, Alix Kates

Drinking the Rain. 1995. Farrar, Straus and Giroux, ISBN 978–0374144036, 241p.

In her fifties, Shulman felt she needed to step back from a hectic life as writer, mother, wife, and feminist. She spent the next 10 summers in a primitive cottage on an island off the Maine coast, discovering the joys of a solitary, slower, simpler lifestyle; her description of that time is intimate, lyrical, and wholly delightful.

Sparks, Nicholas, and Micah Sparks
Three Weeks with My Brother. 2006. Grand Central Publishing, ISBN 0446532444, 356p.

Sparks and his brother Micah took the trip of a lifetime: three weeks visiting the world's most fascinating sites, from Machu Picchu to the Taj Mahal. The only surviving members of their family, they took the time to reconnect and discover the lessons learned from lives filled with tragedy, love, and faith. Fans of bestselling novelist Sparks will find the roots of his stories here.

Stern, Jane
Ambulance Girl: How I Saved Myself by Becoming an EMT. 2003. Crown Publishers, ISBN 140004832X, 228p.

By the time she reached her early fifties, Stern, a successful food writer, was in the grip of debilitating phobias, depression, and panic attacks. Determined to change her life, she signed up for EMT training in her small Connecticut town, enduring the boot camp style classes with humor and determination. Slowly, the lifesaving skills she learned helped her save her own life and gave her the sense of family and community that she craved. Stern pulls no punches about her own fears and mistakes in this heartwarming and very personal story.

Taking It On Faith: Spiritual Journeys

These memoirs from religious seekers appeal to our need for a spiritual dimension in our lives, no matter what faith we profess. These authors all struggled with issues of belief and doubt; their memoirs are refreshingly candid and provocative—even the classic St. Augustine's *Confessions.*

Ahmed, Leila
A Border Passage: From Cairo to America—A Woman's Journey. 1999. Farrar, Straus, and Giroux, ISBN 0374115184, 307p. 📖.

During her childhood in Cairo, the women and children in Ahmed's family gathered daily in her grandmother's salon to eat and tell stories; they also shared their distinctly feminine perception of Islamic law and culture. But by the 1950s, the political and religious climate changed and Ahmed felt estranged there. She left for England, hoping to find a place where Islam and feminism were compatible; her memoir of that search is enlightening, intelligent, and lyrically told.

Braestrup, Kate

⇨ *Here If You Need Me: A True Story.* 2007. Little, Brown and Co., ISBN 9780316066303, 211p. ▭.

Braestrup's life was turned upside down when her husband died in an accident. Left with four young children, she became a chaplain in the Maine Warden Service, helping fish-and-game wardens on search-and-rescue missions, providing comfort and spiritual guidance to families and wardens alike. With humor and compassion, she tells the stories about missing children, suicides, and snowmobile accidents. On the way she muses about religion's answers to life's important questions, and makes her own journey from grief to faith.

Cowan, Paul

An Orphan in History: One Man's Triumphant Search For His Roots. 2002 (1982). Jewish Lights, ISBN 1580231357, 288p. ▭.

Cowan's upbringing as, in his words, "a Jewish WASP," left him with a sense of rootlessness. He embarked on a personal journey to discover the religious, intellectual, and cultural heritage abandoned by the wayside in his assimilated childhood, and to find a way to live as both an American and a Jew. As he retrieved his lost family history and his religion, his life was changed and enriched. Cowan's story is the classic that inspired many others to write about their spiritual journeys.

Hendra, Tony

Father Joe: The Man Who Saved My Soul. 2004. Random House, ISBN 1400061849, 271p. ▭.

As a teenager, Hendra found a mentor and substitute father in the charismatic Benedictine monk Father Joe, who offered him the comfort of God's love without judgment. Although he had a successful career as an editor at *National Lampoon* and writing for British TV, Hendra turned to Father Joe repeatedly when drink and drugs threatened to derail his life. This is a satisfying memoir of spiritual growth: entertaining, heartfelt, and often funny.

Kidd, Sue Monk

The Dance of the Dissident Daughter: A Woman's Journey from Christian Tradition to the Sacred Feminine. 1996. HarperSanFrancisco, ISBN 0060645881, 238p. ▭.

Kidd's spiritual needs literally propelled her out of a comfortable life to find her own way of relating to God, separate from her patriarchal and fundamentalist Christian upbringing. She opens the story with an astonishing anecdote that sets the tone for her search for an authentic feminine religious experience. Readers who enjoyed her novel *The Secret Life of Bees* will gain insight into the sources of her religious beliefs.

Lamott, Anne
Traveling Mercies: Some Thoughts on Faith. 1999. Pantheon, ISBN 0679442405, 275p. 📖.

    Lamott is an engaging writer who doesn't hesitate to reveal her failings: years of drugs and alcohol abuse, married lovers she met in cheap motels, suicidal thoughts. Although she was brought up in a secular household, religion became a lifeline, and when she bottomed out in her twenties, it gave her a way back to believing in herself. Never sentimental, Lamott's take on faith is refreshing and comforting.

Larsen, Deborah
The Tulip and the Pope: A Nun's Story. 2006. Alfred A. Knopf, ISBN 037541360X, 265p.

    Larsen recalls when, in 1960 at the age of 19, she entered a convent in Iowa, so idealistic, so sure her decision was correct. As a postulant, her life and thoughts were reshaped: she learned about obedience and "custody of the eyes," and how to avoid intimate friendships. Brief, episodic chapters, poignant with intimate details of the religious life, tell how her initial peace gave way to doubt and a change of heart about her vocation.

St. Augustine, Bishop of Hippo, trans. by Rex Warner
The Confessions of St. Augustine. 2001 (397). Signet Classic, ISBN 0451527801, 353p. 📖.

    The very first autobiography, Augustine's *Confessions* electrified readers when it was published in 397 A.D. Augustine was the Bishop of Hippo in North Africa and an adult convert to Christianity. The *Confessions* reveals a man struggling and questioning his faith: writing to know himself and understand his God. The surprise here is that at a distance of 16 centuries, Augustine resembles us.

The Ties That Bind: Bittersweet Family Stories

For idyllic family memoirs, look elsewhere; these are complex and unsettling stories about the wounding psychological dramas of family life.

Corrigan, Kelly

The Middle Place. 2008. Voice/Hyperion, ISBN 9781401303365, 262p. 📖.

Corrigan adored her larger-than-life Irish father who lit up every place he went with his exuberance. In her mid-thirties, mother of two young daughters, she was diagnosed with cancer shortly before her own father's cancer recurred. The conjunction of these events brought her to that "middle place" where the roles of parents and children overlap; her warm and funny memoir reminds us of the strength of family bonds.

Eggers, Dave

A Heartbreaking Work of Staggering Genius. 2000. Simon & Schuster, ISBN 0684863472, 375p. AW. 📖.

Eggers was 21 when both his parents died within months of each other, leaving his eight-year-old brother, Christopher, on his own. Although Eggers had two older siblings, he felt responsible. Could he take on the role of parent to a pre-teen and still have a career and social life? Eggers's story of how he reinvented family life in 1990s San Francisco, is engaging and freewheeling, a clever and thoroughly postmodern romp.

Fremont, Helen

After Long Silence: A Memoir. 1999. Delacorte Press, ISBN 0385333692, 319p. 📖.

Fremont's parents were Polish Jews who survived the horrors of World War II, but in the process obliterated their memories and their Judaism, raising their children as Catholics in the United States. It was not until adulthood that Fremont uncovered the truth and finally understood "the hole that lay like an enormous crater" at the center of her family's life. Gracefully and compellingly written, her memoir combines past and present in a beautiful and often terrifying narrative.

Garis, Leslie

House of Happy Endings. 2007. Farrar, Straus, and Giroux, ISBN 9780374299378, 339p. 📖.

Garis's grandparents wrote for the Stratemeyer syndicate, penning series books like *The Bobbsey Twins* and the *Uncle Wiggly* stories, staples of childhood reading in the first half of the 20th century. They all lived together in a beautiful old house in Amherst, Massachusetts, where happiness should have prevailed. But devastating mental illness ravaged the family and Garis's childhood was spent shoring up her emotionally shattered father, while her mother, brothers, and grandmother spun off into their own worlds of pain. A claustrophobic tale of family dysfunction.

Grogan, John
  The Longest Trip Home: A Memoir. 2008. Wm. Morrow, ISBN 9780061713248, 334p.
    Grogan grew up in a Detroit suburb, with loving, devout Catholic parents, who filled the house with saints' effigies, took family vacations to religious shrines, expected their children to attend Mass weekly, and save sex until marriage. His memoir is filled with tender and hilarious stories of how he failed to fulfill his parents' expectations, the emotional cost of their estrangement, and how hard he worked to remain close to them.

Moore, Honor
  The Bishop's Daughter: A Memoir. 2008. W.W. Norton & Co., ISBN 9780393059847, 365p. 📖.
    Moore's father was the charismatic social activist Paul Moore, Episcopal Bishop of the Diocese of New York in the 1970s and 1980s, whose bisexuality ran like a secret current through the lives of his wife and nine children. Moore, the oldest child, probes her parents' letters and interviews old friends in a remarkably literate effort to understand the loneliness and anguish that marked her and her family.

Ondaatje, Michael
  Running in the Family. 1982. W.W. Norton & Co., ISBN 0393016374, 207p. `AW`.
    When Ondaatje returned to Sri Lanka in the late 1970s, he was overwhelmed by memories of the exotic, multicultural, privileged world of his youth. He tells improbable stories of his rakish, irresponsible father and other friends and relatives "who stood in my memory like frozen opera." Ondaatje's impressionistic writing takes the reader deep into a dreamlike world of tropical nostalgia.

Schrand, Brandon R.
  ⇨ *The Enders Hotel: A Memoir.* 2008. Univ. of Nebraska Press, ISBN 9780803217690, 230p.
    Schrand's grandparents owned the crumbling Enders Hotel in Soda Springs, Idaho; it was a refuge for his alcoholic mother and stepfather. For Schrand, it was a paradise of secret store rooms, free meals, and fascinating disreputable guests, an escape from the dark undercurrents of his family life. In sparkling prose, Schrand brings it all to life in a most satisfying memoir of hope and redemption.

Undertow: Edgy, Dark Memoirs

Sometimes we are forever affected by events beyond our control. Skeletons in the closet, illness, deaths, or political upheavals are among the things that can derail lives. For some of these authors, memoir writing was cathartic; it may be cathartic for readers too.

Bloland, Sue Erikson
In the Shadow of Fame: A Memoir by the Daughter of Erik Erikson. 2005. Viking Press, ISBN 067003374X, 229p. 📖.

Bloland's famously charismatic child psychologist father came to prominence in the 1960s with the publication of the groundbreaking *Childhood and Society.* In this memoir, his daughter reveals that at the same time the family lived a life of quiet desperation, with both parents consumed with the search for fame and approval, unable to express warmth toward their children. Their fourth child, born with Down syndrome, was institutionalized and never mentioned. Bloland, herself a psychoanalyst, probes her parents' shortcomings and her own journey to self-understanding.

Brennan, Kate
In His Sights: A True Story of Love and Obsession. 2008. HarperCollins, ISBN 9780061451607, 279p.

When Brennan, a single woman living in the Midwest, began dating wealthy Paul, much was right in their relationship, but Paul's need for emotional and financial control of the women he dated was troubling. When Brennan pulled away, he began to stalk her, using friends and criminal contacts to make her life a nightmare. Brennan fought back and recounts the terrible cost to her sanity and safety.

Brown, James
The Los Angeles Diaries: A Memoir. 2003. Wm. Morrow, ISBN 0060521511, 200p.

Twelve vignettes chart a dark, often harrowing childhood and a dysfunctional adulthood in southern California. Brown recalls waiting in the car as a child while his mother set a building ablaze. Drink and drugs began at an early age; he betrayed everyone around him to feed his addictions. He makes no apologies for the way drug and alcohol abuse made a mess of his family and professional life. Brown's memoir reads like a very dark crime novel.

Franks, Lucinda

⇨ *My Father's Secret War: A Memoir.* 2007. Miramax Books, ISBN 9781401352264, 311p. 📖.

Journalist Franks had plenty of resentment stored up against her distant and bitter father. She suspected that his experiences at the end of World War II, when he was with the first American soldiers to liberate a concentration camp, had scarred him, but felt that there was more to the story. As she researched and probed her father's memory, he slowly revealed that he was a spy, involved in dangerous missions behind enemy lines. As she comes to understand his burdens of secrecy and guilt, they are able to find some healing in their relationship.

Harrison, Kathryn

The Kiss. 1997. Random House, ISBN 067944999X, 207p.

Harrison's memoir was a publishing event: it told of an affair begun at age 20 with the absentee father who haunted her childhood. While she craved the love she never had from him, he gave her something quite different. She recounts their obsessive, painful affair coolly and with remarkable artistry.

Lederer, Katy

Poker Face: A Girlhood Among Gamblers. 2003. Crown Publishers, ISBN 0609608983, 209p.

Lederer grew up on the campus of an East Coast prep school in a family where gambling was the preferred family activity. Her mother was a hard-drinking solitaire player, and her much older brother and sister were high rollers in New York and Las Vegas. Lederer was inexorably drawn into their dissolute orbit for a while; she writes about the nightmarish world of gambling addicts with the insight of an insider.

Shreve, Susan Richards

Warm Springs: Traces of a Childhood at FDR's Polio Haven. 2007. Houghton Mifflin, ISBN 9780618658534, 215p.

Shreve brings a novelist's sensibility to this memoir of her time at Warm Springs Polio Foundation from the age of 11 to 13. A high-spirited tomboy given to breaking rules and acting out, she hoped that the surgeries at Warm Springs would make her a perfect person and heal her melancholy family as well. Shreve's painful, complex coming-of-age story is a poignant glimpse into the way illness shapes our lives.

Index

About the Author

Photo by Gerald Reisner.

ROSALIND REISNER is the author of *Jewish American Literature: A Guide to Reading Interests,* published by Libraries Unlimited and winner of the 2004 Reference Award from the Association of Jewish Libraries. She has worked in public, academic, and school libraries. Rosalind currently writes and speaks about memoirs, Jewish literature, and readers' advisory service. She maintains the website http:// areadersplace.net.

Notes

Notes

Notes